WRITING FOR
WORK
Essential Skills for the Workplace

Mc Graw Hill **Education**

Bothell, WA • Chicago, IL • Columbus, OH • New York, NY

www.mheonline.com

 **Education**

Send all inquiries to:
Contemporary/McGraw-Hill
130 E. Randolph St., Suite 400
Chicago, IL 60601

ISBN: 978-0-07-657792-7
MHID: 0-07-657792-9

Printed in the United States of America.

 2 3 4 5 6 7 8 9 RHR 15 14 13 12

Contents ■ ■ ■

2   Introduction

4   Theme 1: General Workplace Writing

6   Lesson 1: Completing Forms

12   Lesson 2: Communicating News and Reminders

18   Lesson 3: Summarizing Information

24   Lesson 4: Writing Instructions and Guidelines

30   Theme 2: Writing to Supervisors

32   Lesson 5: Expressing Opinions

38   Lesson 6: Making Requests

44   Lesson 7: Responding to Criticism

50   Lesson 8: Raising Concerns

56   Lesson 9: Preparing Reports

62   Lesson 10: Proposing Ideas

68   Theme 3: Writing to Customers and Clients

70   Lesson 11: Informing Customers and Clients

76   Lesson 12: Handling Customer Complaints

82   Lesson 13: Expressing Gratitude

88   Lesson 14: Requesting Payment

94   Theme 4: Writing to Other Organizations

96   Lesson 15: Requesting Information

102   Lesson 16: Offering Feedback

108   Lesson 17: Requesting Meetings

114   Lesson 18: Responding to Queries

120   Job Seeker's Toolkit

122   Create a Personal Fact Sheet

124   Create an Online Profile

126   Create a Résumé

131   Write a Cover Letter

133   Fill Out a Job Application

134   Write a Thank You Letter

135   Write a Follow-up Letter

137   Answer Key

150   Writing Rubric

Common Errors

Introduction ...

Today's employers want employees who have all the skills they need to be successful in the workplace. Having—and being able to apply—academic skills such as reading and mathematics remains important. However, the jobs of the 21st Century require employees to have skills that go beyond these core academic competencies. Employees must also be able to manage themselves, make thoughtful decisions, communicate effectively in writing, and use 21st Century tools to solve problems.

The *Workplace Skills: Essential Skills for the Workplace* series helps you develop competencies that are highly valued in today's knowledge-based economy. Each scenario-based lesson within *Tools for Workplace Success*, *Writing for Work*, and *Applied Computer Basics* focuses on the skills most often identified by employers as keys to career readiness. Lessons also provide opportunities to discuss and apply these skills.

Workplace Skills: Writing for Work ▪ ▪ ▪

In the workplace you will often have to provide information, explain procedures, and effectively communicate your ideas in writing. Since you will also need to be able to adapt your writing to different readers, each theme in this book focuses on a particular audience. The lessons within these themes will help you learn how to write effectively for each type of audience.

Theme 1: General Workplace Writing focuses on day-to-day writing tasks, such as filling out forms, taking notes, and communicating with coworkers.

Theme 2: Writing to Supervisors focuses on writing tasks that are directed to managers and supervisors, such as requesting time off and preparing reports.

Theme 3: Writing to Customers and Clients focuses on writing as the voice of your company, such as when responding to customer complaints and sending updates or other information to clients.

Theme 4: Writing to Other Organizations focuses on various writing tasks, such as requesting information and responding to queries.

Remember!

When you write in the workplace, all of your writing is "for work." Always keep in mind that everything you write in the workplace:

- is a record that will likely stay on file somewhere in the company.
- might possibly be read by your supervisor.
- must be effective in order to achieve the results you seek.
- reflects your effectiveness as an employee, including your intelligence and your level of professionalism.

Making the Most of Each Lesson ■ ■ ■

Each lesson focuses on a group of related writing tasks. Lesson examples and tasks are based on realistic workplace scenarios. All lessons are divided into three sections—Skill Examples, Try It Out, and On Your Own. Each lesson models skills, provides practice, and presents opportunities for you to complete the writing tasks on your own.

Skill Examples To start each lesson, you will read two scenario-based workplace writing examples and analyze the effectiveness of each. By comparing these examples, you will see how factors such as organization, details, clarity, and tone affect the communication.

Try It Out! In this section of the lesson, you will learn how writers plan for and write effective workplace communications using the lesson skills. You will also have a chance to analyze a piece of writing and make revisions.

Regardless of your audience, it is important to plan your writing so that you can communicate clearly and effectively. You can use the *Pre-Writing Plan* to help you organize information before writing:

Pre-Writing Plan			
TOPIC	**PURPOSE**	**AUDIENCE**	**FORMAT**
What do I want to communicate?	What is my reason for writing this?	Who will read what I write?	How can I ensure that this information will get to everyone who needs it?
What information needs to be included?	What do I want the results of this writing to be?	How should I tailor my writing to these readers?	

On Your Own This section of the lesson provides several opportunities for you to apply what you have learned to realistic workplace writing scenarios.

Within each lesson, *Remember!* notes highlight essential foundational skills in grammar, mechanics, spelling, and sentence structure, all of which are important for effective communication.

General Workplace Writing ...

When you write in the workplace, much of your writing will be for coworkers. In fact, you may write to coworkers more often than you write to anyone else. General workplace writing often deals with routine matters, such as completing forms, giving instructions, and passing on important information.

In this section, you will learn the skills needed to communicate effectively when performing general workplace writing.

Lesson 1: Completing Forms Filling out forms requires clear writing, complete information, and an appropriately objective tone. *Tasks include*:

- Completing a Fax Cover Sheet
- Filling Out an Incident Report
- Filling Out a Damage Report
- Accounting for Time
- Filling Out a Delivery Form

Lesson 2: Communicating News and Reminders Writing reminders and sending messages require an understanding of audience, format, and relevant details. *Tasks include*:

- Communicating Safety Issues
- Communicating Security Issues
- Communicating a Disruption of Service
- Providing a Status Update
- Sending a Reminder
- Requesting Cooperation
- Informing Employees of a Requirement

Lesson 3: Summarizing Information Summarizing requires writers to pay attention to details and organization. *Tasks include*:

- Summarizing a Conversation
- Writing a Job Description
- Summarizing an Account of an Incident
- Taking a Phone Message
- Summarizing Guidelines
- Summarizing a Message from a Supervisor

Lesson 4: Writing Instructions and Guidelines Creating instructions and explaining guidelines requires clear language and logical organization. *Tasks include*:

- Detailing a Process
- Writing a Dress Code
- Writing a Code of Conduct
- Writing a New Procedure
- Rewriting Confusing Instructions
- Creating Guidelines

Key Factors for General Workplace Writing ■ ■ ■

You may know your coworkers very well. You may also be very friendly with them. However, this does not mean that writing to coworkers requires less care than writing to a supervisor, a client, or another organization. To write effectively to coworkers, you must communicate clearly, identify important details, organize information logically, and know your audience.

In Theme 1, you will also learn to:

- **Punctuate correctly** Using correct punctuation shows your coworkers that you are careful and attentive to detail. It also demonstrates professionalism and respect for your coworkers.

- **Use correct spelling** Spelling, like punctuation, is a reflection of your professionalism and competence.

- **Choose words effectively** Choosing words carefully can help you communicate clearly and respectfully. Mastering this skill will allow you to represent your company confidently and develop positive relationships with your colleagues.

- **Use correct subject-verb agreement** Using correct subject-verb agreement is important for clear communication. It will also help you develop a professional image.

Knowing how to write to coworkers will increase your effectiveness in your job and demonstrate your professionalism.

Remember!

Effective workplace writing requires a combination of writing skills. However, even a well-crafted message is useless if it does not reach the intended audience. Choosing the right format to communicate your message is essential.

Lesson 1 ▪ ▪ ▪
Completing Forms

You will need to fill out forms for many different types of jobs. When you complete forms, make sure your writing is clear and contains relevant details. Remember that the words you choose affect the tone of your writing. Your language should be formal and professional.

Skill Examples ▪ ▪ ▪

Completing Fax Cover Sheets Rhonda is a real estate agent who needs to fax an important contract to a home buyer at her workplace. The following examples show how Rhonda might complete the fax cover sheet.

Read each example. Then answer the questions that follow.

EXAMPLE 1

FACSIMILE COVER SHEET

To: Accounting Department
Company: Northwood Incorporated
Fax: (215) 555-0157
Pages: 4 (including cover sheet)
Re: sale contract

From: Rhonda Wilson
Company: Real Estate For You
Fax: (215) 555-0184

Hi, here is the paperwork regarding the purchase of you're home. You are seriously getting an awesome deal! Please read the document and call me if you have any questions. Try (215) 555-0199. See you soon.

Rhonda

1. Which of the following questions cannot be answered using the information on Rhonda's fax cover sheet?
   A. Which person is supposed to receive the document?
   B. What document is Rhonda sending?
   C. What company does the home buyer work for?
   D. What agency does Rhonda work for?
   E. What is Rhonda's phone number?

2. Which sentence has an appropriately professional tone?
   F. Hi, here is the paperwork regarding the purchase of you're home.
   G. You are seriously getting an awesome deal!
   H. Please read the document and call me if you have any questions.
   J. Try (215) 555-0199.
   K. See you soon.

Remember!

Spelling It is important to proofread all your workplace writing for correct spelling. Careless mistakes will make your writing less professional and harder to read. In *Example 1*, Rhonda incorrectly writes *you're* instead of *your*. An electronic spell-check might not recognize this error because *you're* could be correct in a different context.

EXAMPLE 2

FACSIMILE COVER SHEET

To: Janelle Morris, Accounting Department   **From:** Rhonda Wilson
Company: Northwood Incorporated   **Company:** Real Estate for You
Fax: (215) 555-0157   **Fax:** (215) 555-0184
Pages: 4 (including cover sheet)
Re: sales contract

Janelle,

Attached is the updated sales contract for the property on Lockview Lane. Please review this document and contact my office at (215) 555-0199 if you have any questions. I look forward to meeting with you again next Tuesday.

Rhonda

3. What would an administrative assistant at Northwood Incorporated most likely do after receiving this fax?

   A. deliver the documents to the head of the Accounting Department
   B. deliver the documents to Janelle Morris
   C. add a Tuesday meeting to Janelle Morris's schedule
   D. contact Real Estate For You to verify that Rhonda Wilson is a real person
   E. throw out the documents because they were faxed to the wrong number

4. How could Rhonda try to convey a more professional tone in her cover sheet?

   F. She could include the price of the home.
   G. She could write *Ms. Morris* instead of *Janelle*.
   H. She could include her home phone number.
   J. She could include the full street address of the home.
   K. She could market her services to other Northwood employees.

Think About It Which example presents information more clearly and professionally? In forming your answer, think about the following questions.

- **Details** What problems could result when important details are not included on a fax cover sheet?

- **Tone** What language choices in the second example succeed in creating an appropriate, professional tone?

Remember!

Capitalization Use correct capitalization when filling out forms. Even a brief form, such as the fax cover sheet in *Example 2*, can create a positive or negative impression. Rhonda correctly capitalizes the names of people (Janelle Morris, Rhonda Wilson); companies (Northwood Incorporated, Real Estate for You); and streets (Lockview Lane). A misspelled name or address can make you appear unprofessional. It can also result in an undelivered or misfiled document.

Try It Out! ▪ ▪ ▪

Filling Out an Incident Report Monique works as an aide at a nursing home. During her last shift, a patient fell out of bed. Monique informs her supervisor about what happened. She also needs to write an incident report for the patient's file.

○○○   **E-mail Message**

To: Yolanda

Subject: Night shift update

Good morning, Yolanda,

I want to let you know that we had a minor incident last night with Mr. Preston in room 318. He fell out of his bed and hurt his arm and hip. (It was nothing serious, just a few bruises.) Mr. Preston forgot to ask for help when he needed to go to the bathroom. I will write up the incident report for his file and leave it on your desk.

Monique

Monique needs to make sure the incident report is clear and accurate. She also needs to include details that explain exactly what happened and any relevant information. She uses the *Pre-Writing Plan* to help her.

Pre-Writing Plan			
TOPIC	**PURPOSE**	**AUDIENCE**	**FORMAT**
Mr. Preston's fall and bruises	To record details of incident	Monique's supervisor	Incident report form

Monique completes an incident report for the patient's personal file.

INCIDENT REPORT

DATE OF REPORT: January 31, 2011   **TIME:** 8:30 A.M.

REPORTING STAFF

Name: Monique Jones   **Title:** Nursing Aide   **Supervisor:** Yolanda Gonzales

DESCRIPTION: At 3:30 A.M., I heard a loud noise in room 318. When I went to investigate, I found Mr. Preston lying on the floor. I asked if he was all right. "Yes," he said, "I bumped my arm, but I think it's okay. I was trying to walk to the bathroom." He said he forgot to buzz an aide for help. I observed some redness on his right arm and right hip. There was no swelling or bleeding.

I helped Mr. Preston to his feet and walked him to the bathroom. Mr. Preston then returned to bed and was asleep as of 3:50 A.M. I checked on Mr. Preston again at 7:30 during the morning shift change. I observed minor bruises on his right arm and hip. However, he said he felt fine. Nurse Kennedy then conducted a patient injury check. She found no injuries.

SIGNATURE OF REPORTING STAFF: Monique Jones

→ **SIGNATURE OF INCIDENT WITNESS (if applicable):** n/a

Remember!

Punctuation If you include a person's quoted words in a report, be sure to punctuate the quote correctly. Monique's description of the incident uses quotation marks to show exactly where each quoted remark begins and ends. End punctuation (commas, periods, exclamation points, and question marks) is usually placed inside the quotation marks.

The writer considers her **audience** when deciding how much detail to offer. She includes important details that her supervisor needs to know.

When writing in this **format**, use *n/a* (which means *not applicable*) to complete any sections that are irrelevant.

Filling Out a Damage Report Anthony is a customer assistant at a party supply store. One day, he accidentally drops a box containing five glass punch bowls. Upon opening the box, he discovers that all five bowls are broken. Anthony must explain how the items were damaged on a damage report form.

Anthony considers the *Pre-Writing Plan* and then explains the cause of damage in the damage report.

INVENTORY DAMAGE REPORT FORM

CAUSE OF DAMAGE

My manager Robert said to move all the punch bowls to the front shelves by tonight. First I was stacking them on the lower shelves. Then I ran out of room. I started stacking the boxes way up high. I had to use a stepladder. Next thing I knew, I totally lost my balance and dropped the box! That got everybody's attention, haha. All of the bowls in that box were broken. I am real sorry. You can take it out of my paycheck if you want.

Write a short response to each item below.

1. Some of the details in the "Cause of Damage" section of the report are unnecessary. Which details could be removed so that this section is focused on relevant information?

2. Consider this sentence: *That got everybody's attention, haha.* This creates the impression that the writer does not take the issue seriously. Rewrite this sentence with a more appropriate tone.

Reflect In the examples on these pages, the writers used the *Pre-Writing Plan* to determine which details to include, how to make the messages clear, and what kind of tone to use. Do you think the examples clearly convey the information? Are the details relevant and sufficient? Does the choice of language establish an appropriate tone?

Remember!
Sequence Words When you recount an incident, include sequence words such as *first, next,* and *then*. That way, the sequence of events is clear to anyone reading your report. In the inventory damage form, the writer effectively uses the sequence words *first* and *then*. He also appropriately uses the sequence word *next,* although the phrase *next thing I knew* is too informal for the report.

On Your Own ▪ ▪ ▪

Read the following scenarios. Then write your own communications based on each scenario.

SCENARIO A Accounting for Time

You are a paralegal for a law firm. Each day, you must complete a work log. It identifies which cases you worked on, how much time you spent on each case, and what tasks you performed for each case. Here is your work log for February 16:

WORK LOG

Date Wednesday, February 16

Case	Tasks	Hours
Otis	Research	2
Otis	Conference call	1
Marshall	Case report preparation	2
Zebrowski	Filing and database updates	3
	Total hours:	8

Complete the *Pre-Writing Plan* below. Then use the work log above to explain how you spent this work day. Your explanation should include sequence words and be in paragraph form.

Pre-Writing Plan			
TOPIC	**PURPOSE**	**AUDIENCE**	**FORMAT**
		Your supervisor	Work log

SCENARIO B Filling Out a Damage Report

You assist customers as a baggage claim agent at a busy airport. Kendra Lipton, a passenger on one of the flights, wants to file a damage claim. Her suitcase was damaged during Happy Skies flight 803 on March 1, 2011. A beverage cart was bumped, knocking over a soda and spilling it over the suitcase's leather exterior. The suitcase is worth $100.

Complete a *Pre-Writing Plan* on your own. Decide which details must be included in the damage report, and then write a paragraph for the report explaining what happened to the suitcase.

SCENARIO C Filling Out a Delivery Form

You are a florist's assistant, and you often take customers' orders over the telephone. You have the following telephone conversation with a customer one morning.

> YOU: *Farbrook Flowers, how may I help you?*
> CUSTOMER: *I'd like to send a Congratulations Bouquet to my niece Tina. She's graduating on June 21st. It's item C-47 on page 35 of your Spring catalog. I want you to use yellow roses instead of pink ones, though.*
> YOU: *That's no problem, sir, and the price will be the same, $25. Could you please tell me your niece's full name, phone number, and address?*
> CUSTOMER: *Tina Trimble, (202) 555-0134, 24 Mayberry Lane.*
> YOU: *And your name, phone number, and billing address, sir?*
> CUSTOMER: *Gary Trimble, (202) 555-0112, 842 Whitman Drive.*
> YOU: *Would you like to include a message on the card?*
> CUSTOMER: *Just "Congratulations, Tina! Love, Uncle Gary and Aunt Sue."*
> YOU: *Great. Finally, do you want us to deliver the flowers on June 21st?*
> CUSTOMER: *Yes, and make sure they get there in the morning.*
> YOU: *Certainly, sir. Thank you for choosing Farbrook Flowers.*

Complete a *Pre-Writing Plan* on your own. Then create a simple delivery form and complete it, explaining the order for the bouquet and giving special instructions.

SCENARIO D Filling Out a Fax Cover Sheet

As the manager of Deb's Diner, you handle food and supply orders. This week, the diner is running low on baked goods. You need to fax an order to Beebee's Bakery. You would like to order five loaves of white bread, five loaves of multigrain bread, three apple pies, and four dozen plain cake doughnuts.

Complete a *Pre-Writing Plan* on your own. Then create and complete a fax cover sheet.

Summary ▪ ▪ ▪

When you are completing forms, remember that your purpose is to communicate accurate information. Additionally, keep these points in mind:

- **Clarity** When filling in forms, be sure to present the information as clearly as possible. Remember that the person reviewing your form may not know who you are or what you do. Being clear helps prevent confusion and mistakes.

- **Details** Include all of the details your audience needs to understand your communication. Forms are designed to provide the audience with important information. This is why it is important to fill in forms carefully and completely.

- **Tone** The way you use language creates an impression, even in short forms. It is important to convey a respectful, professional tone. To do this, avoid informal language and nonstandard usage.

Answers begin on page 137.

Lesson 2 ■ ■ ■
Communicating News and Reminders

In many jobs, you will be asked to communicate important news or reminders to others in writing. When writing these messages, you must consider who needs the information and what the best format is for getting the information to that audience. You must also be sure to include all the important details.

Skill Examples ■ ■ ■

Communicating Safety Issues Lacey is a human-resources assistant at a packaging company. She needs to create an announcement for an office fire drill. She decides an e-mail would be the best way to let all employees know about it. The following examples show how Lacey might write the e-mail.

Read each example. Then answer the questions that follow.

EXAMPLE 1

E-mail Message	
To:	All Employees
Subject:	FIRE DRILL!!!!!

We are going to have the usual fire drill soon and we need to be able to get out of the building in an ORDERLY manner.

Be sure you know how to get out and where to go.

EVERYONE MUST LEAVE THE BUILDING!!!!!

1. Which of the following questions can readers answer using the information in Lacey's e-mail?
   A. When is the fire drill?
   B. How do we get out of the building?
   C. Can anyone stay in the building?
   D. Where do we go after we leave the building?
   E. Why are we having this fire drill?

2. If you scanned this e-mail, reading only the words in all capital letters, what might you think?
   F. Your company will have a fire drill in three days.
   G. The message does not apply to you.
   H. Your office building is on fire.
   J. Everyone needs to leave your building immediately.
   K. Your supervisor will tell you what to do.

Remember!

Capitalization Readers often scan e-mails for important information. Using capital letters and bold fonts can be useful techniques to help readers locate important information. However, if these techniques are overused, they are less helpful and can be misleading. In *Example 1*, Lacey's use of too many capital letters gives the impression that there is an emergency.

EXAMPLE 2

> **E-mail Message**
>
> **To:** All Employees
>
> **Subject:** Company Fire Drill
>
> Please note that a company FIRE DRILL will take place on **Thursday, April 4**. Everyone is required to take part.
>
> - This drill is to ensure that all employees know the exit routes from the building and the outdoor locations of their assembly areas.
>
> - Please respond immediately when the alarm sounds. Walk briskly but do not run to your assembly areas. If you do not know where your assembly area is, ask your supervisor before Thursday.
>
> - Do not re-enter the building until told to do so by your supervisor.

Remember!

Clarity E-mails should be as short as possible while including all necessary information. They should set out the main points so that readers can easily see and understand them all. In *Example 2*, Lacey uses a list with bullet points to clearly communicate the information.

3. Which question cannot be answered based on this e-mail?
   A. On which day will the drill take place?
   B. Can anyone skip the drill?
   C. Why is the drill being held?
   D. Who can tell employees where the assembly areas are?
   E. When was the previous fire drill held?

4. What other information would be appropriate to include in this e-mail?
   F. a detailed history of the company's previous fire drills
   G. the personal contact information for all employees
   H. a link to the company's fire-drill policy
   J. a map of the city
   K. a newspaper article about a recent house fire in the area

Think About It Which example do you feel is more effective? In forming your answer, think about the following questions.

- **Audience** How are techniques such as all capital letters, bold text, underlining, and lists used in each example? Do they make it easy for busy employees to easily find and understand the main points?

- **Details** What information do employees need in order to take part in the fire drill? What details are included in each example?

Try It Out! ■ ■ ■

Communicating a Disruption of Service Tim is a receptionist for a software publishing company. His supervisor left him a voice mail asking him to create a notice concerning the temporary closing of the office cafeteria.

> *Hi Tim, this is Sarah. Good news! We just found out that the cafeteria is going to be remodeled. This means we're going to have more menu choices, faster service, better food, and a much more pleasant atmosphere. We'll also have three more tables and two new pay stations. The problem is, the cafeteria is going to have to be closed for a few days. I'm out of the office this week, so I'd like you to let everyone know about this. Here's the information: It's going to be closed from Wednesday through Friday of next week and will open again the following Monday. While it's closed, employees can use the Main Conference Room between noon and one o'clock for lunch. Thanks a lot, Tim. Give me a call if you have any questions.*

Tim needs to decide which information is important to include in the message. He also needs to decide what kind of format would be best for communicating this information. He uses the *Pre-Writing Plan* to help him.

Pre-Writing Plan			
TOPIC	**PURPOSE**	**AUDIENCE**	**FORMAT**
Temporary closure of cafeteria	To let employees know where they can eat	All employees who use the cafeteria	E-mail and notice

Tim decides that everyone needs to know about this, so he sends an e-mail. He realizes that posting a notice near the entrance to the cafeteria would also help. To be certain people read it, he displays the intended audience prominently.

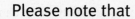

CAFETERIA USERS!

Please note that
the Cafeteria will be CLOSED
from Wednesday, June 6 through Friday, June 8
for remodeling.

On those days you may use
the Main Conference Room for lunch.

We apologize for the inconvenience, but we think you will appreciate the many improvements to come!

Remember!

Tone Using a friendly but professional tone can help readers accept a message, especially a message with negative content. The apology at the bottom of the notice to cafeteria users is a good idea. This can help employees accept the inconvenience and focus on the benefits of the remodeling.

The **audience** is clearly identified at the top of the notice.

This **format** is effective, as long as it is accompanied by an e-mail to everyone in the office.

Providing a Status Update Sergio is a salesperson at a car dealership. He discovers that the dealer's copy machine is not working properly. He calls the Help Line at noon. They tell him that they will send someone to repair the copier within the next three hours. He decides to inform his coworkers of the status of the repair by posting a notice above the copy machine.

Sergio considers the *Pre-Writing Plan* and then writes the notice.

Write a short response to each item below.

1. What additional detail could be added to the last sentence of the notice to make it more helpful to readers?

2. The second sentence of the notice is not helpful if the reader does not know when Sergio wrote the notice. Rewrite this sentence to make it clearer.

Reflect In both these examples, the writers used the *Pre-Writing Plan* to think carefully about the audience and purpose before choosing a format and deciding which details to include. Do you think that the format for each message is appropriate? What other formats do you think would be effective? Did each of the writers include all necessary details?

> ## Copy Machine Users:
>
> The machine is down. I have called the Help Line, and they said they will be here. Within the next 3 hours. If you have any questions, please call the Help Line.
>
> Sergio

On Your Own ▪ ▪ ▪

Read the following scenarios. Then write your own communications based on each scenario.

SCENARIO A Communicating Security Issues

You are a human-resources intern at a chemical company. Your supervisor, Mark, asks you to e-mail all office employees and tell them about recent thefts in area offices. Here is the voice mail that Mark left you.

> *I need you to draft a message for me. Security has notified me of several thefts in area offices. Our office hasn't been hit yet, but we need to tell everyone to be careful. There have been a total of eight thefts in three different office buildings on Capitol Street. All of these have involved purses or briefcases. These usually happened when cubicles were unoccupied during breaks. We need to remind staff that all of our office doors must remain closed so that the automatic locks will activate. I can't understand why people prop these doors open. Also, people need to use the locks on their cubicle cabinets. It's ridiculous not to use these. Tell everyone they should report any thefts to Security. Thanks.*

Complete the *Pre-Writing Plan* below. Then write the e-mail.

| \| Pre-Writing Plan | | | |
TOPIC	PURPOSE	AUDIENCE	FORMAT
		Everyone in office	E-mail

SCENARIO B Informing Employees of a Requirement

You are a restaurant manager creating a rough schedule for the summer. You need all restaurant employees to submit their vacation requests by the end of the week. You posted a notice about this on your office door about a week ago, but several employees did not respond. You think they may not have seen the notice. Now you want all employees to respond, even if they are not requesting time off. You need to create a notice that everyone will see and respond to.

Complete a *Pre-Writing Plan* on your own. Choose the format you feel is most effective. Then create the communication.

SCENARIO C Sending a Reminder

You are a receptionist at a doctor's office. The human resources manager sends you the following e-mail.

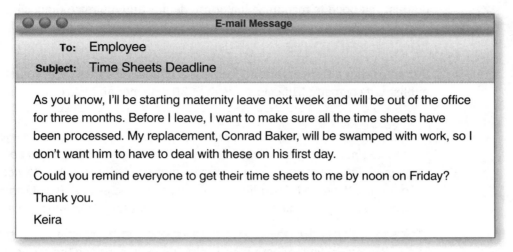

E-mail Message

To: Employee

Subject: Time Sheets Deadline

As you know, I'll be starting maternity leave next week and will be out of the office for three months. Before I leave, I want to make sure all the time sheets have been processed. My replacement, Conrad Baker, will be swamped with work, so I don't want him to have to deal with these on his first day.

Could you remind everyone to get their time sheets to me by noon on Friday?

Thank you.

Keira

Complete a *Pre-Writing Plan* on your own. Choose the format you feel is most effective. Then create the communication.

SCENARIO D Requesting Cooperation

You are an auto mechanic. The refrigerator in the break room of your garage is filthy, and this bothers you. You would like to help by cleaning the refrigerator once a month. You decide to post a notice asking employees to remove their items by Friday, April 23, so that you can clean the refrigerator.

Complete a *Pre-Writing Plan* on your own. Then write the notice.

Summary ▪ ▪ ▪

When you communicate news or reminders, stay focused on your topic and purpose. Additionally, keep these points in mind:

- **Audience and Format** It is not always necessary for every person to get every message. Carefully consider your audience and choose your format wisely.

- **Details** It is important to include all the relevant details in your communications. It is just as important not to include irrelevant details. Do not make readers sift through a message to find the important points.

Answers begin on page 137.

Lesson 3 ▪ ▪ ▪
Summarizing Information

Many writing tasks require workers to take notes and summarize information. To do this, you need to recognize important details and organize them clearly.

Skill Examples

Summarizing a Conversation Sheree is a human resources representative for a publishing company. This morning, the CEO calls her and leaves a message.

> *This is Donna. It's supposed to snow all day and the roads are a mess. Let people know the office is closed. This will affect profits, but it can't be helped. Employees with remote access may work at home, but it's not required. If needed, I can be reached via my home e-mail. People should assume the office will be open tomorrow unless they hear otherwise.*

The following examples show how Sheree might summarize the conversation in an e-mail. Read each example. Then answer the questions that follow.

EXAMPLE 1

⬤ ⬤ ⬤	E-mail Message
To:	All Employees
Subject:	Weather issues

Good morning,

As you may have expected, Donna has decided to close the office today due to the snowstorm. The roads are very dangerous, so be safe and stay home. Our profits will suffer, but I suppose safety is more important.

Sheree

1. Which question cannot be answered based on this e-mail?
   A. Who is sending the message?
   B. Why is the office closed?
   C. Who decided to close the office?
   D. Can employees work from home?
   E. Are the roads dangerous?

2. Which piece of information should Sheree have included in the e-mail?
   F. The snow will continue all day.
   G. There are problems on the interstate highway.
   H. Donna called Sheree this morning.
   J. Donna asked Sheree to e-mail all the employees.
   K. The office is open tomorrow unless employees hear otherwise.

EXAMPLE 2

```
○ ○ ○                    E-mail Message

    To:   All Employees

 Subject:  Office Closed Today Due to Snowstorm
```

Good morning,

Due to the snowstorm, the office will be closed today. Please take note of the following points:

- Employees with remote server access may work from home. However, they are not required to do so.

- Donna can be contacted via e-mail if necessary.

- For now, assume the office will be open for normal hours tomorrow. We will be in touch with you if anything changes.

Enjoy your snow day.

Sheree

3. Which subject line would provide the most clarity for this message?

   A. Snow Day

   B. Weather Issues

   C. Work from Home If You Can

   D. Snowstorm Causes Dangerous Driving

   E. Office Closed Today Due to Snowstorm

4. What additional information would be the most appropriate to include in this e-mail?

   F. Donna's e-mail address

   G. Sheree's home address

   H. a link to the day's weather forecast

   J. a list of local roads that are closed

   K. an estimate of how the lost work day will affect profits

Think About It Which example do you think more effectively summarizes the information? In forming your answer, think about the following questions.

- **Details** If important details are left out of Sheree's e-mail, what problems could result?

- **Organization** How does the organization of each example help make the information clear?

Try It Out!

Writing a Job Description Adrianna works as a library assistant. The library has decided to hire another assistant to help out in the afternoon, which is the library's busiest time of day. Adrianna's supervisor has sent her an e-mail requesting that Adrianna create a job description for a library assistant.

E-mail Message
To: Adrianna Edwards
Subject: Library assistant duties

Adrianna,

I have good news. We will be hiring a new afternoon assistant to work with you. We will post the opening on Monday. Please write up a basic job description that explains a library assistant's responsibilities. We will use this in the job posting. Include just the major duties, like shelving new and returned books, handling interlibrary loan requests, and helping customers with checkouts and returns.

Thank you.

Chris

Adrianna must summarize her major duties and provide enough details so that job seekers will understand the position. She also must make sure her writing is organized. She uses the *Pre-Writing Plan* to help her.

Pre-Writing Plan			
TOPIC	**PURPOSE**	**AUDIENCE**	**FORMAT**
Library assistant's job responsibilities	To list and briefly explain job duties	Job seekers	Job description

Adrianna chooses to create a document that lists and explains her major job duties by category. As Chris has requested, she focuses on three major tasks.

LIBRARY ASSISTANT JOB DESCRIPTION

Major Function: The library assistant help patrons and staff.

Major Duties:

Shelving Books
Shelves new and returned books

Checkouts and Returns
Uses the computerized scanning system to help patrons with checkouts and returns

Interlibrary Loans
Assists guests as needed in completing the paper ILL request forms
Enters formal requests into the Interloan system

Remember!
Subject-Verb Agreement Subjects and verbs must agree with one another in number. Singular subjects take singular verbs, as in *She runs every morning.* Similarly, plural subjects take plural verbs, as in *The books are easy to read.* The subject and verb do not agree in this sentence from the job description: *The library assistant help patrons and staff.* The correct way to write it would be: *The library assistant helps patrons and staff.*

A brief, organized explanation of job duties fulfills the writer's **purpose.**

The writer knows who her **audience** is, so she feels confident that her audience will be familiar with words like *Interloan* and acronyms like *ILL.*

Writing a Job Description A rental car company recently hired Laura as a customer service representative. On her first day, a colleague provides this brief job description:

Customer Service Representative
Job Description

Your primary duty each day is to cover the phone at your work station at all times. This is very important. We never want a situation where customers call and just hear the phone ring. Plan for this when you take breaks.

At the start of each call, ask for the customer's account number. Use it to verify that the information in our computer system is correct. Whenever possible, try to resolve the customer's issue yourself. However, in some cases, you will need to direct calls to a rental agent or to the customer accounts office. (Note: The Employee Training Manual provides guidelines for how you can help customers and when to transfer a call to someone else.)

Throughout the day, maintain the computer log of your phone calls. Record the exact time of each call remember to include the proper code. For example, use numeral 1 for customer questions, 2 for complaints, and 3 for compliments. This helps the company easily see what types of calls we are receiving.

Write a short response to each item below.

1. How could this job description be organized so that Laura's job duties are easier to see and understand?

2. The last sentence of the first paragraph does not give enough information about how breaks are supposed to be covered. Rewrite this sentence, making it clear that customer service representatives are responsible for getting coworkers to cover their workstations during breaks.

Reflect In both these examples, the writers used the *Pre-Writing Plan* to think carefully about the audience and purpose before deciding which details to include and how to organize them. Do you think the organization and details in the examples on pages 20 and 21 fulfill each writer's purpose?

Remember!

Run-on Sentence In the last paragraph of the job description, the second sentence is a run-on sentence. A run-on sentence occurs when two sentences are combined without punctuation or a conjunction. You can fix a run-on sentence by breaking it into two sentences. You can also combine the two sentences with a comma and a conjunction, such as *or, and,* or *but.* The run-on sentence in the job description can be rewritten as two sentences: *Record the exact time of each call. Remember to include the proper code.* It can also be rewritten, using a comma and the conjunction *and: Record the exact time of each call, and remember to include the proper code.*

On Your Own ▪ ■ ▪

Read the following scenarios. Then write your own communications based on each scenario.

SCENARIO A Summarizing an Account of an Incident

In your job as a police officer, you respond to a call about a burglary. The burglary took place at Officeworld Office Supply Store. You have the following conversation with the store manager, Carl.

> *YOU: Could you tell me how and when you discovered the burglary?*
> *MANAGER: When I came in this morning at 7:00, I noticed that the glass on one of our display cases was broken. A large laser printer was missing, along with several boxes of ink and toner cartridges. Someone must have broken in last night.*
> *YOU: Were there any other signs of breaking and entering?*
> *MANAGER: No, not that I noticed. I don't know how they got in.*
> *YOU: Approximately what was the value of the stolen merchandise?*
> *MANAGER: All in all, about $500.*
> *YOU: Thank you, sir. We'll just take a look around to see if we can find out anything else.*

In your investigation, you discover that the back entrance was left unlocked. You conclude that the burglar probably used this entrance. Now you need to write a report with details about the crime.

Complete the *Pre-Writing Plan* below. Then write a description of the incident to use in the report. Use sequence words.

Pre-Writing Plan			
TOPIC	PURPOSE	AUDIENCE	FORMAT
Burglary at Officeworld		Other police officers	

SCENARIO B Taking a Phone Message

You are the office manager for an HVAC (heating, ventilation, and air conditioning) company. One of your customers is the Bright Start Day Care Center on Morningbird Lane. The day care center owner, Carol Myers, calls one morning. She says the air conditioning system is malfunctioning. She says that this morning, the day care was very warm and stuffy, so she turned on the air conditioner. Now the air conditioner will not turn off. No matter how she adjusts the thermostat, there is still cold air coming out of the vents. The children are complaining about being cold. Carol needs the problem fixed immediately, or she will have to close the center for the day. You need to write a message to an HVAC technician describing the problem.

Complete a *Pre-Writing Plan* on your own. Then write a detailed description of the problem to send to the technician.

SCENARIO C Summarizing a Message from a Supervisor

You work for a commercial electrical contractor as an accounts receivable clerk. Part of your job is to contact customers about overdue payments. Your supervisor, Lynn, leaves you a note regarding overdue payments from the Ashland Manor apartment complex. She tells you that the company did electrical work for the apartment complex in January and February. However, the company has still not been paid for the work. Lynn wants you to resend invoices DD0111 and DD0211 along with a letter. In the letter, you should explain that the payment for DD0111 is now 45 days overdue, and the payment for DD0211 is 30 days overdue. You should also tell the complex to disregard the bills if it has already sent in the payment.

Complete a *Pre-Writing Plan* on your own. Then write a letter to Ashland Manor that summarizes Lynn's message.

SCENARIO D Summarizing Guidelines

You stock produce at a grocery store. The store manager calls a meeting with everyone who handles produce to discuss some new food-handling policies. You have been asked to take notes during the meeting. You will use your notes to summarize the new policies. Your summary, based on the following, will be posted in the break room.

> *Thank you all for coming. I just want to go over some new policies to make sure we are following the new food safety guidelines when we handle produce. First, make sure all refrigerated items are stored in the proper refrigerator. No one should store any produce in the refrigerator that is now reserved for meat. Finally, make sure all knives and cutting surfaces are washed thoroughly after each use. Use the green cleaning solution to wash any items. I realize it will take some time to get used to these changes. However, we have to start following these guidelines strictly by next Wednesday.*

Complete a *Pre-Writing Plan* on your own. Then write a summary of the new guidelines based on information presented in the meeting.

Summary ▪ ▪ ▪

When you write a summary, focus on the important points. Additionally, keep these points in mind:

- **Details** Determine which details are important and which should be left out. Make sure any details you include are accurate.

- **Organization** One way to present information clearly is to use time order with sequence words. You can also use bullet points or headings to organize information. This can make your writing easier to understand.

Answers begin on page 138.

Lesson 4 ■ ■ ■
Writing Instructions and Guidelines

An important part of writing for work is knowing how to write instructions. When you write instructions, it is important to organize the information sequentially and to use clear language.

Skill Examples ■ ■ ■

Detailing a Process Reggie is a house painter. His supervisor, Ken, asks him to help train a new employee, Lisa. Reggie must create a list of steps involved in painting a room.

The following examples show how Reggie might write the instructions. Read each example. Then answer the questions that follow.

EXAMPLE 1

PAINTING A ROOM

Gather your supplies. Paint, primer, paint rollers, paintbrushes, ladder, drop cloths, painter's tape, a bucket of water, and rags or paper towels. Measure the room first to know how much paint you will need. Clean the walls using rags and hot water. Then apply a coat of primer. Move and cover the furniture. Also, use drop cloths to cover the floor. Put tape around door frames, baseboards, and windows. Make sure the primer is dry before you apply the first coat of paint. Use rollers for large areas. Use brushes for the corners and hard-to-reach places. Apply 2 or 3 coats of paint, allowing each one to dry. When you are finished, gather and clean your paint supplies. Remove tape and drop cloths. Move all furniture back into place. Then pack up your supplies.

Remember!

Sentence Fragments

Sentence fragments are incomplete sentences. Sentence fragments can confuse the reader because the thought is incomplete. In *Example 1*, the second sentence is not a complete sentence. It is simply a list of painting supplies. One way to correct this fragment is to add the words *You will need* at the beginning of the list of supplies. When you write, be sure to use complete sentences, not fragments.

1. What problem could result if Lisa tried to follow these steps in the order that they were written?
   A. She might gather supplies without knowing how much paint is needed.
   B. She might forget to put tape around the doors and windows.
   C. She might not clean her brushes and rollers after painting.
   D. She might start to apply paint before the primer coat has dried.
   E. She might not bring drop cloths to cover furniture and floors.

2. Which sentence should be the first sentence of the instructions?
   F. Gather your supplies.
   G. Clean the walls using rags and hot water.
   H. Measure the room first to know how much paint you will need.
   J. Make sure you move and cover the furniture.
   K. Make sure the primer is dry before you apply the first coat of paint.

EXAMPLE 2

PAINTING A ROOM

- First, measure the room and calculate how much paint you will need.
- Gather these supplies: paint, primer, paint rollers, paintbrushes, ladder, drop cloths, painter's tape, a bucket of water, and rags or paper towels.
- Move furniture away from the walls.
- Cover the furniture and the floor with drop cloths.
- Put tape around door frames, baseboards, and windows.
- Lightly clean the walls using rags and hot water.
- Then apply a coat of primer and allow it to dry completely. Use rollers for larger areas and brushes for the corners.
- Apply 2–3 coats of paint, allowing each one to dry completely before applying the subsequent coat. Use a wet rag to wipe up stray drips as needed.
- When you are finished, gather most of your supplies. Clean your brushes and rollers. Remove tape and drop cloths.
- Move all furniture back into place once the paint is dry.
- Finally, pack up your supplies.

Remember!
Format Whenever possible, produce documents on a computer, as in *Example 2*, rather than by hand, as in *Example 1*. This creates a more formal and professional document that is more likely to be taken seriously. This also avoids problems that may arise from handwriting that is hard to read.

3. Which part of the process might be unclear to Lisa?

   A. which supplies she will need to gather before painting

   B. where she should place drop cloths before painting

   C. how she should determine whether to use brushes or rollers

   D. which supplies she should gather before cleaning her brushes and rollers

   E. when she should move the furniture back into place

4. What could Reggie do to make the vocabulary simpler?

   F. Replace *supplies* with *materials* throughout.

   G. Replace *clean* with *wash* in the sixth step.

   H. Replace *allow* with *permit* in the seventh step.

   J. Replace *subsequent* with *next* in the eighth step.

   K. Replace *needed* with *necessary* in the eighth step.

Think About It Which example do you think is more effective? In forming your answer, think about the following questions.

- **Organization** What mistakes could a new employee make if the sequence of steps is not clear? How do bullet points and sequence words such as *first* and *finally* make the process clearer?

- **Clarity** What problems could result if the audience does not understand all of the words used in the instructions?

Try It Out! ■ ■ ■

Writing a Dress Code Sheila works in the human resources department of a cable company. She has been asked to write a new field employee dress code. The company has a dress code for office workers. However, there is no dress code for employees who work in the field, such as line installers and repair persons. Sheila will loosely base the new dress code on the following office dress code.

EMPLOYEE DRESS CODE

- Employees may not wear shorts to the office. Skirts must be no shorter than two inches above the knee.
- Sneakers, open-toed sandals, flip-flops, and clogs may not be worn.
- Halter tops, tank tops, off-the-shoulder tops, and T-shirts are not permissible.
- Employees may wear jeans only on Fridays. Jeans must be clean and neat.
- Management reserves the right to modify the dress code as needed.

Sheila must write a dress code that is appropriate for field employees. She uses the *Pre-Writing Plan* to help her.

Pre-Writing Plan			
TOPIC	**PURPOSE**	**AUDIENCE**	**FORMAT**
Dress code for field employees	To explain what field employees should or should not wear	Field employees for a cable company	Dress code

Because of the nature of the work, field employees may wear more casual clothing than office workers. They must also follow safety precautions that do not apply to office employees. Sheila must communicate the dress code clearly.

FIELD EMPLOYEE DRESS CODE

When Working in the Field Employees must wear their protective gear.
- Employes must wear hard hats and work boots when working in high places.
- Employees must wear conductive clothing when working with high-voltage lines.

When Working in the Office Employees may wear certain kinds of casual clothing.
- Employees may wear jeans, T-shirts, and sneakers. Jeans must be clean and not torn or frayed.
- Employees may not wear sleeveless or off-the-shoulder tops.
- Employees may not wear open-toed sandals, flip-flops, or clogs.
- Employees may not wear shorts or skirts.

Remember!

Pronoun-Antecedent Agreement Make sure that each pronoun agrees with its antecedent, or the noun it refers to. Use singular pronouns to replace singular nouns, and plural pronouns to replace plural nouns. Sheila's first sentence is correct because the plural pronoun *their* matches the plural noun *employees.*

The **format** that the writer chooses is important because all field workers need to see the message. In addition to handing out the document, the writer should post it where all field workers will see it. If everyone has a work e-mail address, this document should also be e-mailed.

Listing specific clothing items that are or are not acceptable fulfills the writer's **purpose.**

Writing a Code of Conduct Janet is a self-employed housekeeper. Her clients are pleased with her work and have recommended her to their friends. As a result, she now has more work than she can handle alone, and she hires an employee to help her. Janet needs to create a code of conduct for her new employee. Below is her first draft.

Housekeeper Code of Conduct

1. Show up on time with a positive attitude.
2. Always be on good behavior when interacting with our clients. Remember, everything we say and do makes an impression.
3. Do a good job cleaning every part of the house. Do not leave any assigned tasks undone. Always give the job 100%.
4. Do not waste time or stretch out the work to fill the day. Work quickly and efficiently.
5. Respecting our clients' privacy is important. They give us their trust when they let us into their homes. Never give them a reason to be disappointed in us.

Write a short response to each item below.

1. What could Janet have used in place of numbers to help her organize this code?

2. Vague words such as *good* may not get Janet's point across. Rewrite the first sentence of point 2. Use specific language that helps the reader understand what good behavior is.

Reflect In both of these examples, the writer used the *Pre-Writing Plan* to identify a purpose to clearly communicate to the audience. Do you think the examples on pages 26 and 27 are clear and organized? Are the points presented in a logical sequence?

Remember!

Parallel Structure

When you present items in a list, use parallel structure. This means that the items are grammatically parallel— for example, they are all nouns or all complete sentences. In Janet's code of conduct, each of the points begins with a command except for point 5. To make the structure parallel, the first sentence of point 5 should be rewritten as a command: *Respect our clients' privacy.*

On Your Own ▪ ▪ ▪

Read the following scenarios. Then write your own communications based on each scenario.

SCENARIO A Writing a New Procedure

You work as a front desk clerk in a small hotel. The hotel owner, Charlene, has decided to hire a few bellhops. She asks you to write instructions for them. In the following voice-mail message, she explains how the bellhops will assist the hotel guests with their luggage.

> *Hi, it's Charlene. Our two new bellhops will be starting next week. Their main duty will be to help our guests with their luggage. I'd like you to write a procedure document explaining how they will do this. When guests arrive, bellhops should immediately approach them and offer to assist with their luggage. In particular, they should offer to take any large or heavy items. Bellhops should wait by the front desk as guests check in. Then the bellhops should offer to escort the guests to their rooms. They should load any large or heavy items onto the luggage cart. On the way to the room, bellhops should point out the location of the elevators, dining room, and so on. Once in the room, bellhops should point out the room amenities, such as the TV and thermostat. They should also point out the Hotel Services guide. Lastly, they should ask if the guest has any questions and wish the guest a pleasant stay. Please write up this procedure. Thank you.*

Complete the *Pre-Writing Plan* below. Then write the procedure.

Pre-Writing Plan			
TOPIC	**PURPOSE**	**AUDIENCE**	**FORMAT**
		New bellhops	Procedure

SCENARIO B Detailing a Process

In your job as an event coordinator, you are planning a fiftieth anniversary party for a client. You have also just hired a new assistant. You must explain to her what she should do to help you with the party.

Before the party, your assistant will need to set the tables, sweep the floors, and wipe down the table surfaces. She will also put out floral centerpieces, set up stereo speakers, and greet the guests as they arrive. After the party, she will need to sweep the floor again. She will also remove the stereo speakers, clear the tables, and wrap up any leftover food.

Complete a *Pre-Writing Plan* on your own. Decide how to present the instructions in a logical order. Then choose a format and write the procedure.

SCENARIO C **Rewriting Confusing Instructions**

The museum where you work as a security officer recently installed a new security system. There is a note on the wall next to the security system with instructions on how to use it. However, you find that the instructions are very confusing. You decide to rewrite the instructions. The following is the current version of the instructions.

HOW TO USE NEW SECURITY SYSTEM

To arm system, press * before entering code. To disarm system, press # after entering code. Press # after entering code to arm system as well, but only press * before entering code to arm system, not to disarm it.

Complete a *Pre-Writing Plan* on your own. Then rewrite the instructions for using the security system.

SCENARIO D **Creating Guidelines**

As an office manager at a large warehouse, you supervise an administrative assistant who is in charge of restocking the break rooms with supplies. Lately, the assistant has been slow to restock the break rooms, and employees have been complaining.

You have decided to create formal guidelines for restocking the break rooms. You would like the administrative assistant to restock the first-floor break room every other Monday. All general supplies, such as coffee, tea, and napkins, must be restocked. The break room on the second floor is the most frequently used one. You would like the assistant to restock this break room every Monday.

Complete a *Pre-Writing Plan* on your own. Then write the guidelines.

Summary ▪ ▪ ▪

When writing instructions or guidelines, make sure they will be clear to your audience. To do this, keep the following points in mind.

- **Organization** When you write instructions, aim to make them straightforward and easy for your audience to understand. Use a logical sequence, organize your points with bullet points or numbers, and use sequence words.

- **Clarity** Use specific language and avoid using uncommon terms. This helps ensure that your audience will understand your instructions.

Answers begin on page 139.

Writing to Supervisors ...

In the workplace, you will often need to communicate with your supervisor in writing. For example, you may need to submit a written request to take time off or to adjust your work schedule. In this section, you will learn the skills needed to communicate effectively when writing to supervisors.

Lesson 5: Expressing Opinions Communicating your opinion to a supervisor requires supporting details and a polite, professional tone. *Tasks include*:

- Commenting on a New Procedure
- Responding to a Request
- Providing Feedback on a New Policy
- Responding to Proposals

Lesson 6: Making Requests Successful requests require clarity and effective organization as well as a respectful tone. *Tasks include*:

- Requesting Time Off or a Pay Raise
- Requesting Additional Hours and Resources
- Requesting Clarification
- Requesting Information

Lesson 7: Responding to Criticism Responding to criticism in writing requires carefully organized thoughts and a focused purpose. *Tasks include*:

- Responding to Evaluations
- Responding to Criticism from Customers
- Responding to Rumors
- Responding to Criticism from Supervisors and Colleagues

Lesson 8: Raising Concerns Bringing up concerns to your supervisor requires explanatory details and careful organization. *Tasks include*:

- Raising Safety Concerns
- Raising Concerns about Theft and Misrepresentation
- Raising Quality of Work Concerns
- Raising Concerns about Time Sheets and Record Keeping

Lesson 9: Preparing Reports Writing reports requires sufficient detail and organization to meet your purpose. *Tasks include*:

- Preparing Reports about Employee Performance and Management
- Writing a Report on Malfunctioning Equipment
- Preparing a Customer Complaint Report
- Writing a Report on a New Policy or Process

Lesson 10: Proposing Ideas Suggesting new ideas requires an understanding of your audience and clear, detailed expression. *Tasks include*:

- Proposing New Programs or Additional Employees
- Proposing Changes in Procedures

Key Factors for
Writing to Supervisors ▪ ▪ ▪

Writing to supervisors can be tricky. Some supervisors prefer communications that are short and direct. Other supervisors expect a greater level of formality. Therefore, it is essential that you understand the kind of tone your supervisor expects from you. Even if you are on friendly terms with your supervisor, it is almost always best to use a respectful and professional tone with him or her. To write effectively to supervisors, you must also organize information logically, include only the important details, and write clearly.

In Theme 2, you will also learn to:

- **Avoid run-on sentences and sentence fragments** Using complete and correct sentences shows your supervisor that you pay careful attention to details. It also demonstrates respect for your supervisor.

- **Use transition words and phrases** Transition words and phrases help establish relationships between ideas. Using these words will help your supervisor understand your message.

- **Use proper capitalization** Using correct capitalization, like using complete sentences and transitions, helps make your writing professional and clear. Avoiding capitalization errors also displays your competence as a writer.

Knowing how to write to supervisors can give you an advantage in the workplace. Expressing yourself clearly helps demonstrate your knowledge about your work and your value as an employee.

Remember!

Be careful when writing to your supervisor about controversial or sensitive subjects, such as politics or religion. If your comments are requested, try to keep them objective and unbiased. Never write or forward e-mails that could be considered vulgar or inappropriate.

Lesson 5 ▪ ▪ ▪
Expressing Opinions

Many jobs require that you sometimes express your opinion to your supervisor in writing. When writing these communications, you must use a polite, professional tone. You must also support your views with specific details.

Skill Examples

Commenting On a New Procedure Hannah is a barista at a coffee shop. She wants to provide feedback about a proposed new policy. The following examples show how Hannah could express her thoughts in writing.

EXAMPLE 1

> Tom,
>
>   You proposed a new policy that requires baristas to give receipts to customers or they will receive a free drink. I think this policy might actually interfere with customer satisfaction. Many of our customers want to come in, get their coffee, and leave, without waiting for a receipt.
>
>   Additionally, I am concerned that providing receipts (and free drinks) will slow down service. I think it is unnecessary to change our procedure, and I worry that doing so may decrease customer satisfaction. Thank you for the opportunity to provide feedback on the proposed policy.
>
> Hannah

1. Which of the following phrases expresses Hannah's disagreement most clearly?
   A. You proposed a new policy
   B. I think it is unnecessary
   C. Many of our customers
   D. Thank you for the opportunity
   E. I think this policy

2. What other specific detail could Hannah include to support her point of view?
   F. how many customers she knows by name
   G. how long it takes to replace the receipt paper when it runs out
   H. which food items customers order most frequently
   J. which of her coworkers always give customers receipts
   K. how many customers order more than one cup of coffee

Audience When you write to express your opinion, think about your audience's interests and concerns. Address these in your writing. Hannah understands that as a business owner, Tom wants his customers to be satisfied with the service they receive. In discussing the new procedure, Hannah focuses on how it might affect customer satisfaction.

EXAMPLE 2

Tom,

    Giving free drinks to customers who do not get receipts is a bad idea. People have started to complain about the quality of our coffee. Most people just want to be in and out of the shop quickly they do not want to wait around for a receipt. Filling out receipts is a waste of time. We are already way too busy. Our customers will think this is a crazy idea. Thank you for asking for our opinions.

Hannah

3. Which sentence does not provide relevant information?

   A. the second sentence

   B. the third sentence

   C. the fourth sentence

   D. the fifth sentence

   E. the sixth sentence

4. Which sentence has a polite, respectful tone?

   F. Giving free drinks to customers who do not get receipts is a bad idea.

   G. Filling out receipts is a waste of time.

   H. We are already way too busy.

   J. Our customers will think this is a crazy idea.

   K. Thank you for asking for our opinions.

Think About It Which example more effectively fulfills Hannah's purpose and is more likely to be taken seriously by her audience? In forming your answer, think about the following questions.

- **Details** Do the details in each example support Hannah's opinion?

- **Tone** Think about Hannah's tone in each example. Which example demonstrates a more professional tone?

Remember!

Run-on Sentence Be sure to avoid run-on sentences, which can be confusing. Run-on sentences, like the third sentence of *Example 2*, combine two sentences without using appropriate punctuation or a conjunction. Hannah's run-on sentence could be rewritten as one sentence, like this: *Most people just want to be in and out of the shop quickly, so they do not want to wait around for a receipt.* It could also be written as two sentences, like this: *Most people just want to be in and out of the shop quickly. They do not want to wait around for a receipt.*

Try It Out!

Providing Feedback on a New Policy Eduardo works as a teacher's assistant at a middle school. The principal asks for feedback about a new school policy.

MEMO

To: All Teachers and Teacher's Assistants
From: Principal Martinez

Six months ago, we implemented a new policy for school computer use. All computer use is now monitored. Additionally, social networking sites are blocked.

The goal is to ensure that students stay focused on their schoolwork. I would like help in determining this policy's effectiveness. Please e-mail me with your thoughts on these points:

- how students are using computers in your classroom
- whether you have noticed an improvement in students' work
- whether you have had any problems in enforcing the new policy

Thank you.

Eduardo believes the new policy has been very beneficial. He has noticed a definite improvement in students' work. He wants to share his positive feedback. Eduardo uses the *Pre-Writing Plan* to help him.

Pre-Writing Plan

TOPIC	PURPOSE	AUDIENCE	FORMAT
School policy on computer use	To share thoughts on the policy	Principal Martinez	E-mail

Eduardo wants to provide specific details about the policy's benefits. He also wants to keep his message concise. He focuses on the bullet points in the memo.

E-mail Message

To: Principal Martinez
Subject: School computer-use policy

I think the new policy has had a very positive effect on students' work habits and academic progress. I have definitely noticed an improvement in our seventh-grade social studies class. In response to your questions:

- Our students use computers primarily for research. For example, they research historical topics when writing reports.
- Students' work has greatly improved. When we visit the library, students are focused on the task at hand. In fact, we now maintain a class list of the best websites to go to for researching social studies topics.
- Enforcing this policy has not been difficult. A few students objected, but this problem was short-lived. Most students enjoy using computers for learning.

Remember!

Word Choice When expressing your point of view, it is important that you are clear about your position. Using precise words can help you accomplish this. In the opening sentences of his message, Eduardo uses the words *a very positive effect* and *noticed an improvement*. This helps ensure that Eduardo's agreement with the policy is clear.

Eduardo achieves his **purpose** by clearly stating his opinion at the beginning of the e-mail.

Eduardo stays focused on the **topic** by addressing the specific points the principal asked about.

Providing Feedback on a New Policy Ahmet works as a sales representative for a flooring company. He disagrees with the company's plan to allow employees to dress casually on Fridays.

Ahmet considers the *Pre-Writing Plan* and then writes an e-mail.

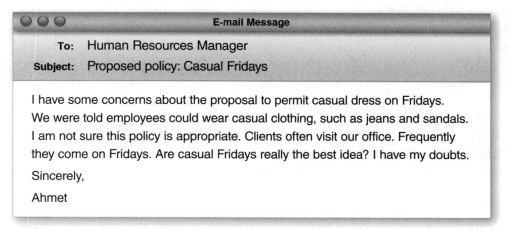

○ ○ ○   **E-mail Message**

To: Human Resources Manager

Subject: Proposed policy: Casual Fridays

I have some concerns about the proposal to permit casual dress on Fridays. We were told employees could wear casual clothing, such as jeans and sandals. I am not sure this policy is appropriate. Clients often visit our office. Frequently they come on Fridays. Are casual Fridays really the best idea? I have my doubts.

Sincerely,

Ahmet

Remember!

Clarity When you express an opinion, it is important to state it clearly and directly. Ahmet does not clearly state how he feels about the new casual Friday policy. He only says that he has concerns about the policy.

Write a short response to each item below.

1. Ahmet's e-mail does not make a clear connection between his opinion and his specific reasons for opposing the policy. What kinds of details could he add to make his message more effective?

2. The third sentence of this e-mail could be viewed as timid or even insincere. Rewrite the sentence to state an opinion that is more professional and clear.

Reflect In both of these examples, the writers used the *Pre-Writing Plan* to think about the best way to achieve their purposes. Which e-mail is more effective? What details, if any, could be added or subtracted to make the e-mails more effective? Is the tone of each e-mail appropriate?

On Your Own ▪ ▪ ▪

Read the following scenarios. Then write your own communications based on each scenario.

SCENARIO A Responding to a Supervisor's Request for More Overtime

You are a technician in a dental laboratory. On Friday afternoon, your supervisor, Brian, sends you the following e-mail.

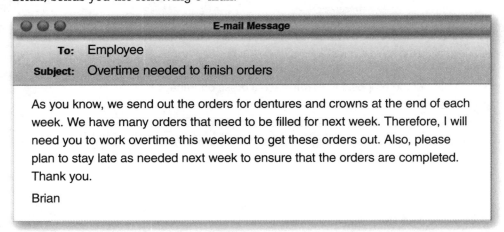

E-mail Message
To: Employee
Subject: Overtime needed to finish orders

As you know, we send out the orders for dentures and crowns at the end of each week. We have many orders that need to be filled for next week. Therefore, I will need you to work overtime this weekend to get these orders out. Also, please plan to stay late as needed next week to ensure that the orders are completed. Thank you.

Brian

You cannot work over the weekend because you will be out of town. However, you can work overtime as needed next week. You must send an e-mail to Brian explaining the situation.

Complete the *Pre-Writing Plan* below. Then write the e-mail.

Pre-Writing Plan			
TOPIC	PURPOSE	AUDIENCE	FORMAT
		Brian, your supervisor	E-mail

SCENARIO B Responding to a New Policy

As a shipping clerk for an online retailer, you have some concerns about a new company policy. Previously, when employees from other departments had free time, they could help the shipping department. This was especially helpful when there were many orders to be filled. However, the new policy states that only shipping clerks can fill orders. You are concerned that the policy will create delays in filling orders, especially during the holidays.

Your supervisor, Lalita, has asked employees for their feedback on the new policy. You want to explain your concerns with it.

Complete a *Pre-Writing Plan* on your own. Decide which format will be most effective and what details you should include. Then write your response.

SCENARIO C Responding to a Proposal to Move to a New Location

You work as an assistant in a pet store. Recently, the store owner called an employee meeting. She announced that she is thinking about relocating the store.

> I called you here today to let you know I am considering relocating the store to Pine Street in the center of town. As most of you know, that area is always very busy. I think we'll have a lot more visibility and more foot traffic. I'd like to hear your feedback. Please take some time to think it over. Then leave a note in the suggestion box. Thanks, everyone.

You do not think this move is a wise idea. You agree with the owner that the new location will have more foot traffic. However, you have some concerns. It would be more difficult for employees to park, and the increased noise on Pine Street could disturb the animals. You decide to share these concerns in your note.

Complete a *Pre-Writing Plan* on your own. Then create the note.

SCENARIO D Responding to a Proposed Rate of Pay

You are an intern at a local radio station. You notice that the station has posted a job listing for an audio technician. You decide to apply for the position since you will be graduating from college next month. A week later, your supervisor sends you an e-mail offering you the job. You are excited. However, you think the proposed salary is not reasonable. The station is offering $25,000/year.

You think that a salary of $30,000/year would be more appropriate. You have previous experience working for your college radio station. In addition, your supervisor knows you are a hard worker. You also know that entry-level salaries for this field are usually more than $25,000. You decide to respond to the e-mail and propose a counteroffer.

Complete a *Pre-Writing Plan* on your own. Then write the e-mail.

Summary ▪ ▪ ▪

When you write to express agreement or disagreement, decide what details to include to express and support your opinion. Additionally, keep these points in mind:

- **Details** Whether you are expressing agreement or disagreement, using specific details and examples will make your writing more effective.

- **Tone** Be polite, but also be clear. When you express disagreement, do so in a respectful manner. You should usually avoid unclear language, such as "I'm not sure if…" or "I kind of think that…."

Answers begin on page 139.

Lesson 6 ■ ■ ■
Making Requests

Many jobs require that you submit certain requests in writing. When you write a request, use a professional and respectful tone. Be sure to include important details. Finally, organize your request so that what you are asking for is clear.

Skill Examples

Requesting Time Off Marion works for a cosmetics manufacturer as a line worker. She needs to send an e-mail to her supervisor, Jane, requesting next Thursday off. The following examples show how Marion might do this.

Read each example. Then answer the questions that follow.

EXAMPLE 1

E-mail Message
To: Jane
Subject: Request for day off
I talked to Carly who usually works the 3:00 to 11:00 shift. Carly said she is willing to work my 7:00 to 3:00 shift. Therefore, my taking this day off will not cause any problems. I will have to take thursday off because I need to take my father to his doctor's appointment.   Thank you.   Marion

1. Which of the following questions can readers answer using the information in Marion's e-mail?

   A. Which Thursday does Marion need to take off?

   B. Why does Marion need the day off?

   C. If Carly covers Marion's shift, who will cover Carly's shift?

   D. Will Marion need any additional time off?

   E. What problems might occur if Marion's shift is not covered?

2. Which change, if any, would make Marion's request clearer?

   F. Leave the sentences as is.

   G. Move the second sentence to the beginning.

   H. Move the third sentence to the beginning.

   J. Move the fourth sentence to the beginning.

   K. Move the fifth sentence to the beginning.

Remember!

Capitalization Even in brief messages, your attention to writing conventions makes an impression. Before you send a request, proofread it to check for any errors. In *Example 1,* Marion did not capitalize the word *Thursday* in her message. This could make her seem careless and unprofessional. This is not the impression an employee wants to give when making a request.

EXAMPLE 2

```
○ ○ ○                    E-mail Message

   To:     Jane

   Subject:   Request to take Thursday off

   I would like to request a day off on Thursday, February 24, due to a family medical
   issue. I spoke with Carly Hanson, who usually works the swing shift from 3:00 to
   11:00. She said she can work my 7:00 to 3:00 shift in addition to her own. My
   station would be covered on Thursday.

   Please let me know if you need any additional information. Thank you.

   Marion
```

3. What information would not be clear to someone reading this e-mail?

   A. the date Marion needs off

   B. which family member is having the medical issue

   C. whether Marion's shift will be covered

   D. whether Carly's shift will be covered

   E. why Marion needs the day off

4. Which phrase conveys a polite, helpful tone?

   F. I spoke with Carly Hanson…

   G. …due to a family medical issue.

   H. …in addition to her own.

   J. My station would be covered…

   K. Please let me know if you need…

Think About It Which example do you think is more effective in making a request? In forming your answer, think about the following questions.

- **Details** What details must be included to ensure that Marion's request is clear?

- **Tone** In which example are the word choices appropriate for a request?

Remember!

Clarity Sometimes writing requests can be difficult. We tend to assume that what is clear to us will be clear to everyone else. To write effective requests, remember to state clearly what you want. In *Example 2*, Marion provides all of the specifics her supervisor needs to understand her request.

Try It Out!

Requesting a Pay Raise Kyle has taught culinary arts at a technical school for one year. He plans to e-mail his supervisor to request a raise. Before writing his message, he writes down his main accomplishments.

> Contributions I have made as a teacher
> - Developed new "Culinary Arts and Customer Service" course.
> - Participate weekly in community outreach program. The program teaches neighborhood children basic cooking skills.
> - Always give 100% to my job. My student evaluations consistently average around 4.8 (out of a possible 5).

Kyle needs to decide which details to include in his e-mail and how best to organize them. He also needs to find the right tone—confident but not pushy. He uses the *Pre-Writing Plan* to help him.

Pre-Writing Plan			
TOPIC	**PURPOSE**	**AUDIENCE**	**FORMAT**
My value as a teacher	To explain why I deserve a raise	My supervisor	E-mail

Kyle decides to include in his message all of the accomplishments he wrote down. This will help make a strong case for a raise.

Presenting accomplishments in a numbered list helps fulfill Kyle's **purpose.**

Because Kyle's **audience** is his supervisor, he conveys respect and enthusiasm for the job.

E-mail Message

To: Ms. Jackson

Subject: Request for a Salary Increase

Dear Ms. Jackson:

In the year that I have been at Tarrytown Technical School, I have greatly enjoyed my job teaching culinary arts. I have proven that I am a valuable member of the team by consistently receiving positive student evaluations, averaging 4.8 out of 5. I am working for the same salary I started at one year ago. I would like to request a pay raise of 5% ($2,500/year). I have contributed to our school in two ways.

1. In response to student and faculty feedback, I developed a new course, "Culinary Arts and Customer Service." This filled a gap in our curriculum.

2. Every week I participate in our "Kids Can Cook" community outreach program. My students teach basic cooking skills to students at our local middle schools. As a result, this program is raising our profile in the community. My students also say teaching others is improving their own learning.

Thank you for your consideration.

Kyle

Requesting Additional Hours Mason has worked part-time as a dry-wall installer for six months and considers himself a valuable employee. He plans to write to his supervisor requesting more hours.

Mason considers the *Pre-Writing Plan* and then writes a note.

Hi, Conrad,
Well, I've been here for six months now. Working with you guys is super fun! I think
I have shown that I am a total stand-up guy who can be depended on no matter what.
I work hard and consistently try to improve my skills. I would really like to get some
more hours. Ten more hours a week would be awesome. Let me know if that works
for you. Thanks in advance for thinking about it.
Mason

Write a short response to each item below.

1. Which words or terms should be revised to make Mason's request sound more professional?

2. The third sentence of the message uses informal language. Rewrite this sentence with more appropriate language.

Reflect In both of these examples, the writers used the *Pre-Writing Plan* to help them choose the right details and tone for their particular purpose and audience. Do the examples present relevant details in an organized way? Is the tone appropriate for requesting something from a supervisor?

Remember!

Punctuation

Exclamation points show strong feelings, such as anger or excitement. By adding an exclamation point at the end of the second sentence, Mason shows that he enjoys working with his coworkers a lot. In formal writing, it is often best to avoid using exclamation points. These can make it seem like you are shouting,

On Your Own ▪ ▪ ▪

Read the following scenarios. Then write your own communications based on each scenario.

SCENARIO A Requesting Clarification of Instructions

You have recently been hired as a paralegal at a law firm. One of the lawyers leaves a voice mail for you. The lawyer asks you to review information for a case, organize it, and write a report.

> *Hi, it's Kendall. I need you to put together a report on the Armstrong case. You can get all of the relevant files from the team that's been working on it. Review the information carefully and use our standard template to organize it. Then send it through the usual reviewers. Please have the report to me before our next meeting with the client. Thanks.*

As a new employee, you are not familiar with the procedure for preparing reports. You also have no information about the Armstrong case. To ensure that you can perform the assigned task, you need to ask Kendall some questions. You decide to write a list.

Complete the *Pre-Writing Plan* below. Then write the list of questions.

Pre-Writing Plan			
TOPIC	PURPOSE	AUDIENCE	FORMAT
	To obtain information needed to perform task correctly	Kendall	

SCENARIO B Requesting Additional Resources

You are a bill collector for a collection agency. Your supervisor gives you a long list of past-due accounts to follow up on by the end of the week. You realize that the task is too large for you to complete on time. However, you think it would be manageable if you had someone else's assistance for four hours a day through the end of the week. You decide to request additional help.

Complete a *Pre-Writing Plan* on your own. Decide what information to include, how to organize it, and what tone is appropriate. Then write the request.

SCENARIO C Requesting Time Off

As employees at a fast-food restaurant, you and your coworkers work variable shifts. Your supervisor, Amanda, allows employees to trade shifts as long as all shifts are covered. One day you arrive at work and find the following notice on the bulletin board. It is from your coworker, Liz.

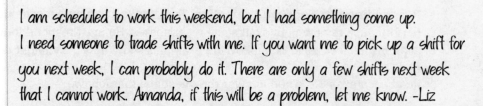

NEED TO TRADE SHIFTS

I am scheduled to work this weekend, but I had something come up. I need someone to trade shifts with me. If you want me to pick up a shift for you next week, I can probably do it. There are only a few shifts next week that I cannot work. Amanda, if this will be a problem, let me know. -Liz

That weekend, you notice that Liz is working her scheduled shift because no one switched with her.

Think about how you would have written the notice if you were in Liz's place. Complete a *Pre-Writing Plan* on your own. Then write the notice.

SCENARIO D Requesting Information about a Job Opportunity

You are an administrative assistant for a marketing company. Recently you learned that your company has an opening for a market researcher. You are considering applying for the position. First, however, you would like to e-mail the head of the research department to get more information.

Complete a *Pre-Writing Plan* on your own. Then write the e-mail.

Summary

When you write a request to your supervisor, make sure the communication is appropriate for your audience. Additionally, keep these points in mind:

- **Details** Include enough details to support your main points. To keep your communication easy to read, leave out unnecessary details.

- **Organization** Emphasize your main points at the beginning and/or the end of your message. Use sequence words and transition words to connect ideas. When presenting lists, organize them using numbers or bullet points.

- **Tone** Your tone for workplace requests should be positive, respectful, and professional—especially when writing to a supervisor. Avoid informal language. Use polite phrases, such as *I would appreciate*, and say *please* and *thank you.*

Answers begin on page 140.

Lesson 7
Responding to Criticism

In most jobs, your supervisor will evaluate your work performance, which could include criticism. When you respond to criticism, you must organize your thoughts carefully. Be sure to maintain an objective, professional tone, and stay focused on your purpose, which is to make a difficult situation better.

Skill Examples

Responding to a Negative Evaluation Troy works as an auto mechanic. His performance review points out some weaknesses. He must respond to his supervisor's feedback. The following examples show how Troy might do this.

Read each example. Then answer the questions that follow.

EXAMPLE 1

EMPLOYEE EVALUATION

EVALUATION (to be completed by supervisor)

Rating: Needs Improvement

Comments: Troy's technical skills are quite satisfactory, and he generally does high-quality work. However, Troy needs to be more professional. His work area is frequently untidy, and he has arrived late several times. He can display a negative attitude by complaining about customers. Troy needs to improve in these areas.

RESPONSE (to be completed by employee)

I do not really see what the issue is here. I was hired to fix cars, not clean. I will admit that I have been late a few times. When the buddy I ride with was late picking me up. My attitude isn't perfect, but people care about whether their cars run, not whether we smile. I respect you and I do like it here, so I will try to do better.

1. What question cannot be answered based on Troy's response?
   A. How does Troy feel about his supervisor?
   B. Why has Troy been arriving to work late?
   C. Does Troy acknowledge that his performance has some weaknesses?
   D. What will Troy do to try to improve his performance?
   E. Does Troy want to continue working at this job?

2. What tone does Troy use in the first two sentences of his response?
   F. He sounds irritated and argumentative.
   G. He sounds unconcerned and happy.
   H. He sounds apologetic and willing to change.
   J. He sounds worried about losing his job.
   K. He sounds concerned about what others are saying about him.

Remember!

Sentence Fragment

Sentence fragments, such as the fourth sentence of Troy's response, can confuse readers. They can also make you appear unprofessional. One way to fix a sentence fragment is to combine it with another sentence in the same paragraph, like this: *I will admit that I have been late a few times when the buddy I ride with was late picking me up.* Another way to fix a fragment is to rewrite it as a complete sentence: *This happened when the buddy I ride with was late picking me up.*

EXAMPLE 2

EMPLOYEE EVALUATION

EVALUATION (to be completed by supervisor)

Rating: Needs Improvement

Comments: Troy's technical skills are quite satisfactory and he generally does high-quality work. However, Troy needs to be more professional. His work area is frequently untidy, and he has arrived late several times. He can display a negative attitude by complaining about customers. Troy needs to improve in these areas.

RESPONSE (to be completed by employee)

I appreciate your positive feedback about my skills and the quality of my work. I will work to improve my performance in the other areas you mentioned. First, I will set aside a little time at the end of each day to make sure my work area is neat. I will also deal with my transportation situation, which has been the cause of my occasional late arrivals. Most importantly, I will work on my attitude. Thank you for giving me the opportunity to improve. I will not let you down.

3. Which topic should Troy have explained in more detail?
   A. his technical skills
   B. the quality of his work
   C. his untidy work area
   D. his lateness
   E. his negative attitude

4. Troy begins and ends his response with positive comments. He addresses his problems in the middle of the paragraph. What is the effect of using this organizational structure?
   F. It avoids discussing any of Troy's weak points.
   G. It helps the audience focus on Troy's strong points.
   H. It shows that Troy's weaknesses are not his fault.
   J. It shows that the supervisor's criticisms are not accurate.
   K. It emphasizes the good qualities that Troy's supervisor did not mention.

Think About It Which example is more effective in responding to negative feedback? In forming your answer, think about the following questions.

- **Tone** What tone or attitude should you try to convey when responding to criticism? What tone should you avoid?

- **Organization** How does the organization of these examples affect the quality of Troy's writing? How does Troy use organization to better respond to criticism?

Try It Out!

Responding to Rumors of Poor Performance Yvonne is a cashier for a home improvement store. Her coworker, Bill, shares an upsetting rumor with her.

> *Yvonne, I heard that your register was missing twenty dollars. If I were you, I would try to be a little more careful. I'm not saying you did anything wrong, but everyone's been talking about it. I also heard that your supervisor is going to give you a warning. You might want to figure out how you're going to explain this.*

Remember!

Punctuation Commas make sentences easier to understand by grouping words and phrases together. In the second paragraph of her note, Yvonne should have placed a comma after *If my register has come up short.* Without the comma, the sentence is confusing.

Yvonne wants to talk with her supervisor, Kenzie, as soon as possible to clear up the rumor. However, Kenzie is not at work today. Yvonne decides to communicate with Kenzie in writing. She uses the *Pre-Writing Plan* to help her.

Pre-Writing Plan			
TOPIC	PURPOSE	AUDIENCE	FORMAT
A rumor about missing money	To request a meeting to discuss the situation	Supervisor	Note

Yvonne decides to leave a note on Kenzie's desk requesting a meeting. That way, Kenzie will see it immediately when she returns.

The **topic** is identified in the first sentence.

The note briefly summarizes the issue and focuses on Yvonne's **purpose**— arranging a meeting.

Dear Kenzie,

I would like to meet with you to discuss some recent rumors I heard about how I have been handling the money in my register. Today a colleague told me that he had heard my register was missing twenty dollars. He had also heard that you were planning to warn me about the missing money.

This was the first I had heard of any problems with my register. If my register has come up short finding the cause of the discrepancy would be important. Perhaps we can work on this together.

This colleague also said that everyone is talking about this, so I would like to dispel any rumors as quickly as possible.

Please let me know when we can meet. I will be here from 8 to 4 all week, and I can also meet with you before or after my shift. Thank you.

Yours truly,

Yvonne

Responding to Rumors of Poor Performance Alex, a bus driver, hears a rumor that his supervisor, Miguel, is upset with him. People are complaining that Alex does not stop at designated bus stops.

Alex considers the *Pre-Writing Plan* and writes a note to Miguel.

Hey, Miguel,

I heard from Trevor that you're not thrilled with my work lately. I can explain this situation. I am not trying to upset anyone. See, sometimes the bus is totally packed and there is no room for any more passengers. If no one on the bus ask to be dropped off, I keep driving. Apparently people complain because I don't always stop at every bus stop. I am not trying to pass anyone by on purpose. Anyway, if you think we need to hash this out some more, just give me a ring.

Thanks,

Alex

Write a short response to each item below.

1. How could the sentences in this note be reorganized so that the specific problem is clear from the beginning?

2. The terms "hash this out" and "give me a ring" in the last sentence are informal and unprofessional. Rewrite this sentence to convey a tone that is appropriate for this situation and audience.

Reflect In both examples, the writers used the *Pre-Writing Plan* to carefully consider the organization and tone of their communications. Is each message organized effectively? Which language choices affect the tone of each message?

Remember!

Subject-Verb Agreement Proofread all communications for grammatical errors. Be sure you are using singular verbs with singular subjects and plural verbs with plural subjects. Alex's note contains an error in subject-verb agreement (*no one … ask*). This error can distract readers and cause them to take the message less seriously. Alex should rewrite the sentence correctly: "If *no one* on the bus *asks* to be dropped off, I keep driving."

On Your Own ▪ ■ ▪

Read the following scenarios. Then write your own communications based on each scenario.

SCENARIO A **Responding to Criticism from a Customer**

As a receptionist for a roofing company, you routinely speak with customers. One afternoon, someone from the repair crew lets you know they are running late and will not make it to the last scheduled job. You try to contact the customer to reschedule, but no one answers when you call. The next morning, the company's voice mail has a complaint from the upset customer. You need to e-mail your supervisor to explain the situation and ask how to handle it. Below is the customer's voice mail.

> *This is Bob Caldwell. I am very upset with your company right now. Yesterday your repair crew was scheduled to come fix a leak in my roof. I waited all afternoon and no one showed up. I was home the whole time, working outside in the garden, so there is no way I would have missed them. There had better be a good explanation for this. I don't appreciate having my time wasted.*

Complete the *Pre-Writing Plan* below. Then write the e-mail to your supervisor.

Pre-Writing Plan			
TOPIC	PURPOSE	AUDIENCE	FORMAT
		Your supervisor	E-mail

SCENARIO B **Responding to Criticism from a Supervisor**

As a bookkeeper for a local grocery store, you have occasionally been slow in depositing money into the store's account. The store owner sends you an e-mail stating that late deposits are unacceptable. You want to apologize. You also want to propose having a set procedure for depositing money in the future. For instance, you could agree to deposit it by 10:00 A.M. the next business day.

Complete a *Pre-Writing Plan* on your own. Decide how to organize the ideas and convey the right tone. Then write the e-mail.

SCENARIO C Responding to Criticism from a Colleague

You work as a nurse aide at a nursing care facility. A colleague confronts you one evening about not cleaning the kitchen right after dinner. You explain that you prefer to clean it after residents have gone to bed. Your coworker says this is not your supervisor's preference. You want to talk with your supervisor to clarify what the best procedure is. Your supervisor will not be in until after your shift ends. You decide to leave her a note.

Complete a *Pre-Writing Plan* on your own. Then write the note.

SCENARIO D Responding to Criticism from a Customer

You are a sales associate in the luggage department at a department store. One day a customer approaches you. She is looking for an inexpensive, medium-sized suitcase. Hoping to make a big sale, you show her an expensive option first. The customer gets upset and leaves the store. Later she sends the e-mail below to the customer-service department. You need to write a note to your supervisor to respond to the complaint.

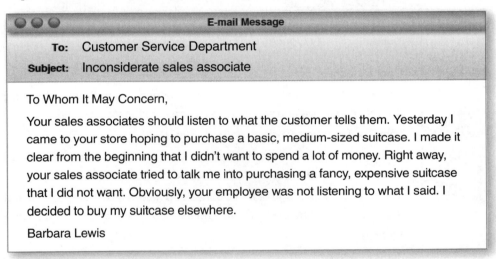

> **E-mail Message**
>
> **To:** Customer Service Department
> **Subject:** Inconsiderate sales associate
>
> To Whom It May Concern,
>
> Your sales associates should listen to what the customer tells them. Yesterday I came to your store hoping to purchase a basic, medium-sized suitcase. I made it clear from the beginning that I didn't want to spend a lot of money. Right away, your sales associate tried to talk me into purchasing a fancy, expensive suitcase that I did not want. Obviously, your employee was not listening to what I said. I decided to buy my suitcase elsewhere.
>
> Barbara Lewis

Complete a *Pre-Writing Plan* on your own. Then write the note to your supervisor.

Summary ▪ ▪ ▪

When you respond to criticism, your goal is to explain the situation and propose a way to fix the problem. Additionally, keep these points in mind:

- **Tone** Avoid sounding defensive or emotional. Use a neutral, objective tone.

- **Purpose** Do not make the mistake of focusing too much on an explanation rather than a solution. Your main purpose in responding to criticism is to help resolve the problem.

- **Organization** Use a problem-solution structure to organize your response. Briefly sum up the problem. Then present your solution.

Answers begin on page 141.

Lesson 8 ▪ ▪ ▪
Raising Concerns

In most jobs, you will occasionally need to raise concerns with your supervisor. When writing to raise concerns, you should include explanatory details. You should also organize your writing carefully.

Skill Examples ▪ ▪ ▪

Raising Safety Concerns Jimmy is a road maintenance worker for a small town. He wants to write an e-mail to his supervisor expressing concerns about worker safety. The following examples show how Jimmy might do this.

Read each example. Then answer the questions that follow.

EXAMPLE 1

E-mail Message
To: Darrell Jones
Subject: Safety Concerns

Dear Mr. Jones:

I think the Town Council should purchase reduced-speed signs. These signs are not very expensive and would not be a strain on the town's budget.

I have some safety concerns and recommendations.

Drivers rarely slow down as they pass my crew on Main Street, and they frequently exceed the speed limit. This is dangerous. We are doing repair work.

There is also a shortage of traffic cones and reflective vests. I recommend that the Town Council reassess the budget for these items and adjust it as needed.

Sincerely,

James Farley

1. Which question cannot be answered based on the e-mail?
   A. What is Jimmy concerned about?
   B. What is Jimmy's job title?
   C. Do reduced-speed signs cost a lot of money?
   D. Is roadwork being done?
   E. Where is Jimmy's crew working?

2. Which sentence should be at the beginning of the e-mail?
   F. sentence 1
   G. sentence 2
   H. sentence 3
   J. sentence 4
   K. sentence 5

Remember!

Parallel Structure Use parallel structure within sentences. For instance, in a series of verbs, use the same verb form. Jimmy correctly wrote, "Drivers rarely *slow down* as they pass my crew on Main Street, and they frequently *exceed* the speed limit." He could also have written, "I have noticed drivers rarely *slowing* down as they pass my crew on Main Street and frequently *exceeding* the speed limit."

EXAMPLE 2

```
●  ●  ●                    E-mail Message

   To:    Darrell Jones

   Subject:  Safety Concerns

Dear Mr. Jones:

As a road maintenance worker for Pinesboro, I am writing to discuss issues that
could affect worker safety and to propose solutions for these concerns.

My road crew is currently doing repair work on Main Street. I have noticed that
drivers frequently exceed the posted speed limit and rarely slow down as they
pass us. This could endanger our crew. Therefore, I propose that the Town
Council purchase reduced-speed signs. These could be posted on busy
thoroughfares when crews are doing work.

In addition, our department is in need of new equipment. There is a shortage of
traffic cones and reflective vests. Some workers purchased these items on their
own because they are so important to safety. I recommend that the Town Council
reassess the budget for these items and adjust it as needed.

I would appreciate your sharing these suggestions with the Town Council.
Thank you.

Sincerely,

James Farley
```

3. Which question cannot be answered based on this letter?

   A. What is dangerous about the situation on Main Street?

   B. How long will Jimmy's crew be working on Main Street?

   C. What action does Jimmy want his supervisor to take?

   D. What roadwork safety items are in short supply?

   E. How have crew members tried to cope with equipment shortages?

4. How would you describe Jimmy's tone in his letter?

   F. calm and informal

   G. appropriately angry

   H. serious and reasonable

   J. overly worried

   K. timid and uncertain

Think About It Which example expresses Jimmy's concerns more effectively?
In forming your answer, think about the following questions.

- **Organization** What is the best way to organize Jimmy's e-mail?

- **Details** What details are included in each example to support Jimmy's
  concerns?

Remember!

Transition Words
Transitions show relationships between ideas and help make your writing flow. This helps the reader follow your thoughts. For example, Jimmy inserted the transition *In addition* at the beginning of his third paragraph. This transition helps join ideas from one paragraph to another. Other ways to transition between paragraphs include *furthermore, similarly,* and *however.*

Try It Out! ■ ■ ■

Raising Concerns about Theft Alberto stocks shelves in a toy store. He and his coworker, Stacey, have the following conversation about a possible shoplifting.

> *ALBERTO: Hey, Stacey, didn't we just restock the bins in aisle 12 last night? Those bins have all the small toys, like little stuffed animals.*
> *STACEY: Yes, we restocked them. Why do you ask?*
> *ALBERTO: Amy told me to check that aisle and restock any bins that need it. I checked and some of the bins are nearly empty. I do not think we sold that many toys in a day. That merchandise doesn't usually sell that fast.*
> *STACEY: That doesn't sound good. I wonder what's going on.*
> *ALBERTO: Maybe we have a shoplifting problem.*
> *STACEY: You know, it's possible. Those bins are way back where the lighting isn't very good. It would be easy for a person to steal small items.*
> *ALBERTO: I'm going to write an e-mail to Amy about it. Maybe we can move those bins to a different place.*

Alberto needs to decide which details to include in his note and how to organize them. He uses the *Pre-Writing Plan* to help him.

Pre-Writing Plan

TOPIC	PURPOSE	AUDIENCE	FORMAT
Possible shoplifting from aisle 12 bins	To discuss shoplifting and offer a suggestion	Supervisor	E-mail

Alberto does not know for sure that shoplifting is occurring. However, he decides to include the suggestion to move the bins to deter potential shoplifters.

E-mail Message

To: Amy

Subject: Potential Shoplifting

Dear Amy,

I'm concerned that customers may be shoplifting items from the small-toy bins in aisle 12. I have not witnessed any actual shoplifting. However, I've noticed that items in the bins seem to disappear very quickly. For instance, I refilled the bins on Monday night, and by Tuesday afternoon, several bins were nearly empty. I have not seen many customers buying these toys.

Additionally, the bins are in a poorly lit area. We might want to consider moving the bins to the front of the store. That way, we can easily monitor them.

Alberto

Remember!

Spelling Contractions are made when a verb and another word are joined together. For example, in the first sentence of his e-mail Alberto combined *I* and *am* to create *I'm*. In the third sentence, he joined *I* and *have* to create *I've*. Contractions mimic the way people speak and are fine for informal writing. However, they are not appropriate for formal written communications.

Because Alberto is not completely certain about the nature of the problem, a brief e-mail is an appropriate **format** in which to communicate his concerns.

Alberto's **audience** is his supervisor, so he does not tell her what to do. Instead, he makes a polite suggestion.

Raising Concerns about Theft Lian is a salon hairstylist who suspects another stylist of stealing. She decides to send an anonymous e-mail to her supervisor through the salon's website.

Lian considers the *Pre-Writing Plan* and then writes the e-mail.

E-mail Message

To: Salon Manager

Subject: Theft by Employee

You may have a problem with theft during my shifts. I think I have seen my coworker stealing things on at least two occasions.

The first time, it looked like she had shampoo, styling gel, and several other kinds of items in her purse. The shampoo I saw in her bag was the 10-ounce, green bottle for normal hair. The gel was from the new all-natural hair care line we just got in. At no point during the shift did I see her pay for those items.

The second time, her pockets were really full. Earlier in the day, I saw her looking at the small tubes of gel. I think there were less tubes in the bin after that. I bet they were in her pocket. I am not positive, so I do not want to give you her name. I just want to bring it to your attention.

If I were you, I would keep an eye on everyone. Maybe we should do a bag check before anyone is allowed to leave the salon. That would make it hard for people to get out of the store with stolen products. I forgot to mention that the first time I also saw my coworker with a hairbrush with a purple handle and a black headband that still had the tags attached to them.

Write a short response to each item below.

1. Which sentence in the last paragraph provides information that belongs in the second paragraph?

2. The first sentence is not helpful if the reader does not know when the writer works. Rewrite this sentence to include this information.

Reflect In both *Try It Out!* examples, the writers used the *Pre-Writing Plan* to help them choose details to include in their e-mails. Are these communications effective? Do they include the necessary details? Are they organized in a way that makes it easy to follow the main points and details?

Remember!

Word Choice Using words correctly in your writing shows that you pay attention to details and are professional. Be especially careful when using commonly confused words, such as *less* and *fewer*. In the third sentence of her e-mail, Lian writes: "I think there were *less* tubes in the bin after that." This is incorrect. She should have written: "...fewer tubes in the bin." *Fewer* should be used to modify nouns that can be counted, such as *tubes*. On the other hand, *less* should be used to modify nouns that cannot be counted, such as *gel*.

On Your Own ▪ ■ ▪

Read the following scenarios. Then write your own communications based on each scenario.

SCENARIO A Raising Quality of Work Concerns

You are a security guard at a hospital. You are concerned that other security guards are often distracted playing with their smartphones. You discuss the problem with a friend who works as a security guard at a mall.

> YOU: I hate to say it, but I think some of my coworkers barely notice what's going on at the hospital. They're too busy playing with their smartphones all the time.
>
> FRIEND: Yes, we have the same problem at the mall where I work. The guards get bored, so they're always sending text messages and playing games.
>
> YOU: I understand why they do it, but it's definitely a distraction. In this job, we need to be observant all the time. What if a patient wandered off the grounds while a security guard was busy checking her e-mail? We also need to respond immediately when there's a problem. Just a few seconds of delayed reaction time could matter a lot.
>
> FRIEND: I agree. Maybe you should talk to your supervisor about it.
>
> YOU: Yes, I think I'll write her a note.

Complete the *Pre-Writing Plan* below. Then write the note.

Pre-Writing Plan			
TOPIC	**PURPOSE**	**AUDIENCE**	**FORMAT**
Distracted security guards			Note

SCENARIO B Raising Concerns about Misrepresentation

As a salesperson at a bridal shop, you are concerned about a potential miscommunication with customers. Recently, the store posted a sign advertising "Same-Day Alterations." However, some alterations are very time-consuming. Because of this, the store's seamstress can complete alterations on only one dress per day. Several customers have complained to you. They say the sign is misleading. You decide to write a note to your supervisor stating your concerns and suggesting that the sign be taken down or changed.

Complete a *Pre-Writing Plan* on your own. Decide what details to include and how to organize them. Then write the note.

SCENARIO C Raising Concerns about Time Sheets and Record Keeping

You are a furniture mover for a delivery company. Employees are required to complete time sheets for each day they work. Most of your coworkers wait until the end of the week to fill these out. You are concerned that this may be causing inaccuracies. You have had several conversations like this:

> *COWORKER: I never remember to keep up with this sign-in sheet. Let's see, on Monday I worked from 7:00 to 3:00. Do you remember when I came in on Tuesday?*
> *YOU: I don't know. Around 7:00 or 7:30, maybe.*
> *COWORKER: Let's just call it 7:00. Okay, so we'll say I worked from 7:00 to 3:00 on Tuesday, Wednesday, Thursday, and today.*
> *YOU: But didn't you leave early yesterday?*
> *COWORKER: Well, yes, but I'll just make up the extra hour today or next week or something. It all evens out in the end.*

You decide to write to your supervisor. You will suggest a new timekeeping policy requiring all employees to fill out time sheets daily rather than weekly.

Complete a *Pre-Writing Plan* on your own. Choose the format you feel is most effective. Then create the communication.

SCENARIO D Raising Safety Concerns

You work as a server in a small restaurant. You are concerned about the door to the kitchen that swings in both directions. On several occasions, you have almost been hit in the face by the door when someone has opened it suddenly. Several coworkers agree that this is a problem, especially when they are carrying drinks, hot food, or heavy trays. You decide to write a note to the restaurant manager. You will explain the problem and suggest a solution.

Complete a *Pre-Writing Plan* on your own. Then write the note.

Summary ▪ ▪ ▪

When you write to discuss concerns, present your concerns clearly and with as much detail as necessary. Offer some possible solutions. Keep these points in mind:

- **Details** Include specific details to show why the issue is a problem or could become a problem. If you are offering a suggestion, include specific details.

- **Organization** State your concern in the opening sentences of the communication. By doing so, you will help your audience understand the details that follow.

Answers begin on page 142.

Lesson 9
Preparing Reports

Many companies have standard forms that employees are expected to use for reports. Other companies expect employees to write the reports on their own. To be effective, your reports must be organized and include enough details to fulfill your purpose.

Skill Examples

Preparing an Employee Performance Report As a quality control inspector for a clothing manufacturer, Randy recently trained a new coworker, Sanjay. Randy's supervisor asks him to write a peer report evaluating Sanjay's performance. The following examples show how Randy might write the report.

Read each example. Then answer the questions that follow.

EXAMPLE 1

EMPLOYEE PERFORMANCE REPORT

Employee: Sanjay   **Evaluator:** Randy

Date: March 1, 2011

Summarize the employee's strengths and weaknesses below.

Sanjay is becoming a valuable employee overall. He is a team player, always willing too help out in a crunch. Additionally, his quality of work is consistently excellent. Sanjay shows attention to detail, even in busy periods like last month.

Sanjay needs to improve his speed and efficiency so that he can process a higher volume each day. Most days, he does not complete as much work as other inspectors. He processes about 80% of the volume of work that others typically complete. He also needs to learn how to adapt to challenging situations, such as when we had to fix incorrectly stitched blouses last month.

1. Which question cannot be answered based on this report?
   A. What are Sanjay's strengths as an employee?
   B. What are Sanjay's weaknesses as an employee?
   C. Does Sanjay finish as much work as the other workers do?
   D. How will Randy help Sanjay improve his performance?
   E. What is Randy's overall assessment of Sanjay as an employee?

2. How is the summary organized?
   F. The first paragraph gives main points; the second gives examples.
   G. The first paragraph gives examples; the second gives main points.
   H. Both paragraphs discuss strengths and weaknesses.
   J. The first paragraph gives strengths; the second gives weaknesses.
   K. The first paragraph gives weaknesses; the second gives strengths.

Remember!

Spelling Homophones are words that sound the same but have different spellings and meanings, such as *to, too,* and *two. Example 1* includes a homophone error in the second sentence. The phrase "willing *too* help out" should be changed to "willing *to* help out." Because many spell-check programs will not catch these errors, it is important to proofread your writing carefully. Some often confused homophones are *it's/its, they're/there/their,* and *site/cite/sight.*

EXAMPLE 2

EMPLOYEE PERFORMANCE REPORT

Employee: Sanjay   **Evaluator:** Randy

Date: March 1, 2011

Summarize the employee's strengths and weaknesses below.

Sanjay is quickly becoming a very useful addition to our department. He is dependable and cooperative and pays attention to detail.

Sanjay, along with all of us, were seriously challenged last month due to a high volume of quality control problems. An entire shipment of women's blouses were incorrectly stitched. The seams had single-needle stitching rather than our standard double-needle stitching. This problem would have had a huge impact on durability if we had not caught it. Sanjay helped us make some of the repairs.

There are some aspects of the job Sanjay needs to work on, but overall he is doing fine. Unfortunately, I cannot say the same for our manufacturing department. In addition to the issue described above, we have been noticing problems with uneven dye and buttons coming loose. With all of these problems, you cannot blame us for processing items slowly.

3. Which piece of information is not clear based on this summary?
   A. Sanjay's strengths
   B. Sanjay's value as an employee
   C. the specific aspects that Sanjay needs to work on
   D. the type of stitching needed on the blouses
   E. the challenges the quality control department has faced

4. In the last paragraph, Randy loses track of his purpose. Which sentence from that paragraph, if any, belongs in the report?
   F. none
   G. sentence 1
   H. sentence 2
   J. sentence 3
   K. sentence 4

Think About It Which example do you think is more effective as an employee evaluation? In forming your answer, think about the following questions.

- **Organization** How does Randy organize his reviews? Does he stay focused on the topic throughout both evaluations?

- **Details** In which example does Randy include unnecessary details that do not belong in Sanjay's evaluation? What important details does Randy leave out?

Remember!

Subject–Verb Agreement When you write, make sure that your subjects and verbs agree in number. In *Example 2*, the subjects and verbs do not agree in two places in the second paragraph. The subject of the first sentence is *Sanjay*, which is singular. Therefore, "*Sanjay*, along with all of us, *were*" should be changed to "*Sanjay*, along with all of us, *was*." The subject of the second sentence is *shipment*, which is also singular. The correct way to write the sentence is: "An entire *shipment* of women's blouses *was* incorrectly stitched."

Try It Out! ■ ■ ■

Writing a Report on a New Policy Justin is a customer service representative for a bank. His supervisor sent him an e-mail asking him to write a brief report about a new policy that was implemented one month ago.

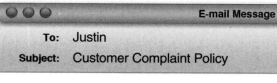

E-mail Message

To: Justin

Subject: Customer Complaint Policy

As you know, we recently set up a new policy for handling customer complaints. When a customer complains, the bank issues a letter thanking the customer for his or her feedback. We also let the customer know that the bank will investigate the complaint. Letters must go out within 72 hours of receiving the complaint.

Please create a brief report summarizing how your department is implementing the policy. Include details about the volume of complaints and customer feedback, if any. Also include any other relevant information. Thank you.

Jonathan Chao

Branch Manager

Justin needs to decide what details to include in this report and how to organize it. He uses the *Pre-Writing Plan* to help him.

Pre-Writing Plan			
TOPIC	**PURPOSE**	**AUDIENCE**	**FORMAT**
Implementation of Customer Complaint Policy	To summarize how policy has been implemented	Branch manager	Report

Since his manager asked for a brief summary, Justin decides to focus on the requested information. Justin will use headings to organize the information.

COMPLAINT-POLICY REPORT

To: Jonathan Chao   **From:** Justin Evans

Date of Report: May 3, 2011

➤ **Summary** In April 2011, the bank instituted a policy of responding by letter to all customer complaints. Letters thank customers for their feedback and inform them that the bank is investigating their complaints.

Processing Volume We processed 40 customer complaints during the last month. Sixty percent of those calls occurred between April 23 and April 30. The high volume may have been due to problems with our online system.

Customer Feedback Three customers wrote to thank the bank's representatives for responding to their complaints promptly.

Remember!

Capitalization Proper names should always be capitalized. In the Complaint-Policy Report, *Justin Evans* and *Jonathan Chao* are capitalized because they are proper names.

Justin's report uses the "To:" field to clearly state the intended **audience**.

Justin includes a summary paragraph to fulfill his writing **purpose**.

Writing a Report on a New Process Harry is a receptionist for a pest control company. He must write a report on the process used for handling customer complaints.

Harry considers the *Pre-Writing Plan* and writes the report.

PROCESS REPORT: ADDRESSING CUSTOMER COMPLAINTS

Authored by: Harry Hanson

Date of Report: May 6, 2011

Currently we have no standard process for handling customer complaints. Someone calls with a complaint. I usually write it down on a sticky note. This can create problems. I suggest that we establish an official process.

The current process is disorganized and inefficient. Sometimes important information gets buried under my usual pile of paperwork and then forgotten. (I apologize, but these things happen.) Because I am the only one who handles the phones, all complaints come in to me. I just write down what the customer says on a sticky note. I know this is not the most organized way to handle it. However I am also multitasking and handling many other duties throughout the day, such as directing calls and greeting visitors.

I think we should replace the current process of using sticky notes with a more formal one. The company should create a standardized form for recording customer complaints. It could be either a printed form or a spreadsheet. This would make it much easier for a busy receptionist to keep complaints organized. That way we could address them more quickly and thoroughly and improve customer satisfaction.

Write a short response to each item below.

1. Which sentences in the second paragraph provide relevant information?

2. The first paragraph contains short sentences, which makes the writing choppy. Use *when* to combine the second and third sentences. Use *so* to combine the fourth and fifth sentences.

Reflect In both examples, the writers used the *Pre-Writing Plan* to help them decide which details to include and how best to organize them. How do the details and the organization make each message more effective or less effective?

Remember!

Tone The tone of a report should be objective and impersonal. Even if you are presenting very positive or negative news, use a neutral tone. Harry's tone is overly negative. In addition, he makes the report personal by making apologies and focusing on his own shortcomings.

On Your Own ▪ ▪ ▪

Read the following scenarios. Then write your own communications based on each scenario.

SCENARIO A Writing a Report on Malfunctioning Equipment

You work as part of the technical support team for a medium-sized information technology business. Recently, your team has been overwhelmed with calls from colleagues. Some of these calls should be directed to other staff. Your supervisor, Kelsey, leaves you a voice mail with suggestions for addressing this problem. You must create a report summarizing the information in Kelsey's voice mail.

> Hi, it's Kelsey. I have some suggestions about how we can handle the misdirected calls our team has been receiving, and I'd like you to create a report on it. Right now about 50 percent of our calls are legitimate. They concern problems with the office communications network. Anyone experiencing communications problems should contact our team by calling the help desk at extension 4567. However, we should not be handling problems with office equipment, such as copier and printer malfunctions. Those issues make up 20 percent of our calls! We need to let employees know that they should contact Rob at extension 4601 for those kinds of problems. Finally, many employees have had trouble with the online time-tracking system. That issue makes up about 30 percent of our calls. Consuela in Human Resources is in charge of that system. She can be reached at extension 4444. If she cannot fix the problem, she will contact us. Please write a brief report summarizing these points and send it to me for approval. Thanks a lot.

Complete the *Pre-Writing Plan* below. Then write your report.

Pre-Writing Plan			
TOPIC	PURPOSE	AUDIENCE	FORMAT
Misdirected calls to Tech Support			Report

SCENARIO B Preparing an Employee Performance Report

As a receptionist for a recording studio, you answer the phone and perform various clerical tasks. Three months ago, the company hired a temporary employee to assist you. The company is now considering hiring this employee full time. Your supervisor has asked you to write a brief report evaluating her performance. You consider the employee friendly and professional and think she makes a good impression on callers and visitors. She also has a very positive attitude. Occasionally, however, she is disorganized when performing clerical tasks, such as making copies or distributing mail.

Complete a *Pre-Writing Plan* on your own. Decide what details to include to fulfill your purpose and how best to organize those details. Then write the report.

SCENARIO C **Preparing a Customer Complaint Report**

You just started working for the customer service department of a trucking company. Part of your job is to write detailed monthly reports that summarize complaints from customers and the general public. Last month you received five calls regarding Vehicle #A45162. Callers complained that the vehicle was speeding. You also received two calls about Vehicle #B7892, complaining that the driver was drifting into another lane. One customer, Greene's Groceries, complained that two of its deliveries were late. You received no complaints about damaged goods.

Complete a *Pre-Writing Plan* on your own. Then complete the report.

SCENARIO D **Preparing an Employee-Management Relations Report**

You are a correctional officer. Your supervisor has asked employees to write a report identifying ways to improve employee-management relations. Your notes are below.

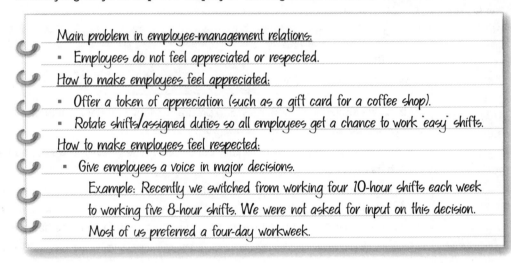

Main problem in employee-management relations:
- Employees do not feel appreciated or respected.

How to make employees feel appreciated:
- Offer a token of appreciation (such as a gift card for a coffee shop).
- Rotate shifts/assigned duties so all employees get a chance to work "easy" shifts.

How to make employees feel respected:
- Give employees a voice in major decisions.
  Example: Recently we switched from working four 10-hour shifts each week to working five 8-hour shifts. We were not asked for input on this decision.
  Most of us preferred a four-day workweek.

Complete a *Pre-Writing Plan* on your own. Then write the report.

Summary ■ ■ ■

When you prepare reports, include information that fulfills your purpose, and organize this information carefully. Additionally, keep these points in mind:

- **Organization** When you create reports on your own, be sure to use headings and subheadings to organize information clearly.

- **Details** Include general statements summarizing your main points. Support these points with specific details.

Answers begin on page 142.

Lesson 10
Proposing Ideas

Many jobs provide opportunities for employees to propose new ideas. When you propose an idea, think about how to make it seem worthwhile to your audience. Explain your idea clearly and provide sufficient details.

Skill Examples

Proposing a Company Recycling Program Faye works for an insurance company as a data entry clerk. She wants to propose a recycling program for the company. The following examples show how Faye might do this.

Read each example. Then answer the questions that follow.

EXAMPLE 1

E-mail Message

To: Carla

Subject: Recycling Proposal

I think we should institute a recycling program. Many companies find that recycling boosts morale and saves money at the same time.

Employees who are environmentally conscious are less likely to waste resources, such as paper.

We could put recycling bins in every office for various items. We could even look into whether it is possible to implement single-stream recycling. An employee would not have to separate their items—everything would go in the same bin.

I would like to discuss this idea with you. Please let me know when would be a convenient time to meet. Thank you.

Faye

1. Which question can readers answer using the information in this e-mail?
   A. How expensive would it be to implement the recycling program?
   B. How many companies in this industry have recycling programs?
   C. How do other employees feel about implementing a recycling program?
   D. How would implementing a recycling program benefit the company?
   E. Which items would be recycled?

2. How does Faye ensure that her audience will be interested in her proposal?
   F. She uses *please* and *thank you*.
   G. She sends her message by e-mail.
   H. She identifies her topic in the subject line.
   J. She stresses how the proposal will help the company.
   K. She asks to meet to discuss the idea.

Remember!

Pronoun-Antecedent Agreement This proposal contains an agreement error between a pronoun and its antecedent (the noun the pronoun refers to). The noun *employee* is singular, and the pronoun *their* is plural. In this case, the best solution is to make both the noun and pronoun plural, as in "*Employees* would not have to separate *their* items—everything would go in the same bin."

EXAMPLE 2

E-mail Message

To: Carla

Subject: Recycling Proposal

I have an idea for a change that might benefit our company. It will definitely be hard at first, but I think we should go forward anyway. I think we should institute a company-wide recycling program.

I think employees would accept this idea. Some of them are environmentally conscious and do this already. I also think employees would be happy to see more plants around the office.

I suggest that we consider putting recycling bins in every office. It would probably be easy to do. I hope that you will implement this proposal by next month. Even if it costs you money at first.

I also think it would be a good idea to encourage people to carpool to work.

Faye

---

3. Which question can be answered based on this e-mail?

A. How many reams of paper does the company use each month?

B. How could implementing Faye's idea improve business?

C. What would Faye like her supervisor to do in response to this note?

D. Which items would be recycled?

E. How much will it cost to implement the proposal?

4. Which sentence might discourage the audience from accepting the proposal?

F. sentence 1

G. sentence 2

H. sentence 3

J. sentence 4

K. sentence 5

Think About It Which example do you feel is more effective? In forming your answer, think about the following questions.

- **Details** Which details should be included to interest the audience and help them understand the proposal? Which details are irrelevant?

- **Audience** Which example shows a better understanding of what is important to the audience?

Try It Out! ▪ ▪ ▪

Proposing a Training Program Reggie is an account collector for a credit card company. He thinks new employees need better training. His notes are below.

> ### Why We Need a Formal Training Program
> - Legal aspects of collection are complicated. It's important for employees to have at least a basic understanding of federal and state laws before they start.
> - They need to know about bankruptcy laws.
> - Credit CARD Act of 2009 introduced many changes.
> - On-the-job training is not the best way to learn.
> - I learned this way and made many mistakes at first.
> - Currently the "learning curve" affects new employees' productivity.
> - Mistakes could pose a legal risk for the company.

The purpose of Reggie's proposal is to get his supervisor to understand the benefits of a formal training program. He needs to decide how to present his idea clearly and convincingly. He uses the *Pre-Writing Plan* to help him.

Pre-Writing Plan

TOPIC	PURPOSE	AUDIENCE	FORMAT
Formal employee training program	To explain how a formal training program would benefit the company	Supervisor	Proposal

Reggie must decide which details to include to make his proposal appealing.

PROPOSAL: TRAINING PROGRAM

Authored by: Reggie Nguyen **Date:** May 1, 2011

Summary Formal training could improve efficiency and reduce legal risks.

Current Training New employees currently learn through "on the job" training. This is not the most effective system because it takes about six months to learn all the aspects of the job. New employees are not familiar with all relevant federal and state laws, which poses potential legal risks.

Proposed New Training and Anticipated Benefits New employees could benefit from first undergoing a week-long training program on legal issues, such as bankruptcy and changes resulting from the Credit CARD Act of 2009.

After the training, employees would be paired with mentors for six months. Mentors would assist employees with any unusual situations. This system would reduce the risk of new employees accidentally violating the law.

Next Steps I would like to meet to discuss this proposal further. Should you decide to implement a training program, I would be happy to help develop it.

Remember!

Sequence Words

When you present a list of reasons or steps, consider using sequence words to organize the list. Reggie uses the words *first* and *after* to introduce different parts of the proposed training.

Reggie's **audience**, his supervisor, is likely to care about efficiency and legal risks, so Reggie addresses these issues.

Reggie fulfills his **purpose** by explaining specific benefits of the proposed new training program.

Proposing a Training Program Tammy is the only employee at a pet store who knows how to conduct obedience classes. She would like to train the other employees in how to do this. She decides to send the store owner a proposal.

Tammy considers the *Pre–Writing Plan* and then writes the proposal.

PROPOSAL FOR TEACHING EMPLOYEES TO TRAIN DOGS

Summary: Due to Summerville's new laws, we have seen a marked increase in requests for obedience training. Instead of recruiting new talent, I propose offering Pet Trainer Classes for some of our current employees.

Objective: As you know, the Summerville shelter has recently switched to a no-kill philosophy. As a result, their are now pit bulls and Dobermans in the shelter.

Dog owners must be able to control there dogs on a leash. Dogs such as pit bulls and Dobermans require extra training. The request for dog-training sessions has nearly doubled. I cannot handle this alone, so we have been turning customers away.

Solution: I have contacted other professional pet-care trainers. They are too busy to take on even part-time work. Few other qualified trainers are in the area.

I propose spending two weekends to train other employees in dog training. In particular, Annie and Dave have good instincts and, with the right instruction, could hold their own dog-training classes in a matter of weeks.

Please let me know what you think. I will be available on Monday and Tuesday if you would like to meet to discuss.

Tammy

Write a short response to each item below.

1. Tammy does not directly state the main benefit. What is it?

2. Combine the second and third sentences in the third paragraph, using the word *since.*

Reflect In both of the examples, the writers used the *Pre–Writing Plan* to help them choose important and relevant details for their audience. What details could be added to make the proposal clearer or to appeal to the audience's interests?

On Your Own ▪ ▪ ▪

Read the following scenarios. Then write your own communications based on each scenario.

SCENARIO A Proposing a Maintenance Procedure

You are a receptionist at an optometrist's office. Recently you have noticed that the waiting room often looks untidy. Magazines are scattered about, and the water cooler is frequently empty. After getting a drink of water, patients sometimes crumple their paper cups and leave them on the tables. You would like to propose an afternoon cleaning plan. You also suggest purchasing wastebaskets for the waiting area. You make these suggestions in a proposal to the office manager.

Complete the *Pre-Writing Plan* below. Then write the proposal.

Pre-Writing Plan			
TOPIC	**PURPOSE**	**AUDIENCE**	**FORMAT**
		Office manager	Proposal

SCENARIO B Proposing a Process Change

You deliver documents as a messenger for a law firm. One of your friends is a messenger for another company. You have the following conversation with your friend.

> *FRIEND: These electronic signature pads are fantastic. My company just bought them for all of the messengers. Once someone signs the pad, the device automatically transmits the signature to the designated file.*
> *YOU: So it's like when you sign for a package and the parcel service automatically records that you received it.*
> *FRIEND: Yes, it works the same way. At first it was tricky to use, but now I don't have to waste time looking through a stack of papers for the right document to give someone. Plus it means our administrative staff doesn't have to spend as much time making photocopies. It also cuts down on our paper consumption.*
> *YOU: Are there any disadvantages?*
> *FRIEND: Well, as I said, it did take me a few days to get comfortable using the device. Also, the best models cost four to five hundred dollars. If a company has a lot of messengers, switching to electronic signature pads would be expensive. Of course, if your delivery is time-sensitive and the signature device malfunctions, it could be a big problem.*
> *YOU: Interesting. Maybe I'll submit a proposal to my boss to see if she'd be interested in that.*

Complete a *Pre-Writing Plan* on your own. Then write the proposal.

SCENARIO C Proposing Safety Ideas

As a landscaper, you work outdoors for most of the day. Sunburns, insect bites, and stings are everyday hazards. You and your coworkers currently buy your own sunscreen and insect repellent. However, this is becoming expensive. You would like the landscaping company to supply these items and issue protective clothing to block out the sun. You decide to submit a proposal to the company owner.

Complete a *Pre-Writing Plan* on your own. Then write the proposal.

SCENARIO D Proposing Additional Employees

You are a meat cutter at a poultry processing plant. Work has gotten much busier, and you think that the plant should hire more workers. You want to propose the idea to your supervisor. Your notes are below.

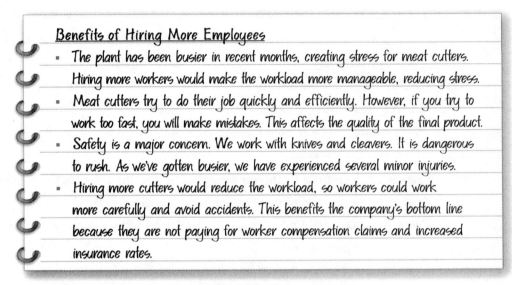

Benefits of Hiring More Employees
- The plant has been busier in recent months, creating stress for meat cutters. Hiring more workers would make the workload more manageable, reducing stress.
- Meat cutters try to do their job quickly and efficiently. However, if you try to work too fast, you will make mistakes. This affects the quality of the final product.
- Safety is a major concern. We work with knives and cleavers. It is dangerous to rush. As we've gotten busier, we have experienced several minor injuries.
- Hiring more cutters would reduce the workload, so workers could work more carefully and avoid accidents. This benefits the company's bottom line because they are not paying for worker compensation claims and increased insurance rates.

Complete a *Pre-Writing Plan* on your own. Then write the proposal.

Summary ▪ ▪ ▪

When you propose an idea, your purpose is to convince your audience to consider your idea. Additionally, keep these points in mind:

- **Details** Include details about how the proposal would benefit the organization. You might also explain why the current way of doing things is problematic.

- **Audience** Remember, you are trying to "sell" your idea. Think about what your audience cares about and tailor your proposal to those issues.

- **Clarity** Explain the idea adequately and consider having another person read your proposal to make sure it is clear.

Answers begin on page 143.

Writing to Customers and Clients ...

When you communicate in the workplace, you will often need to write to customers and clients. Your communications must demonstrate your professionalism and also reflect your company's interests.

In this section, you will learn the skills needed to communicate effectively when writing to customers and clients.

Lesson 11: Informing Customers and Clients Communicating with customers and clients requires careful selection of format, details, and tone. *Tasks include*:

- Notifying Customers about Improvements in Service
- Notifying Customers about Increased Delivery Charges
- Informing Customers about a Change of Address
- Notifying Customers about Billing and Payment Rules
- Notifying Clients of New Business Hours
- Notifying Clients about Retirement

Lesson 12: Handling Customer Complaints Handling complaints requires a clear statement of the problem, a solution, and details. *Tasks include*:

- Recording Complaints
- Acknowledging Receipt of a Complaint
- Responding to Complaints

Lesson 13: Expressing Gratitude Thanking customers or clients requires a warm and professional tone, an appropriate format, and clearly expressed thoughts. *Tasks include*:

- Writing a Thank You Note
- Thanking a Client for a Referral
- Acknowledging a Customer's Appreciation
- Showing Appreciation of Customers
- Writing a Recommendation
- Creating a Personal Thank You Card
- Creating a Postcard to Show Appreciation

Lesson 14: Requesting Payment Asking for payment requires a respectful and professional tone in addition to organized and relevant details. *Tasks include*:

- Sending an Invoice
- Sending a Payment Reminder
- Writing a Form Cover Letter
- Writing a Request for Payment
- Writing a Payment Reminder
- Sending a Second Payment Request
- Explaining an Invoice

Key Factors for Writing to Customers and Clients ▪ ▪ ▪

Writing to clients, like writing to supervisors, requires the ability to apply the appropriate tone depending on the client and the circumstances. You need to know your audience. A professional and respectful tone is always appropriate, even when writing to clients you are on friendly terms with. To write effectively to customers and clients, you must also be able to identify important details, organize information logically, and choose the right format.

In Theme 3, you will also learn to:

- **Spell and punctuate correctly** Using correct spelling and punctuation is very important when writing to customers and clients. Many customers will view your spelling and punctuation as a reflection of the care and quality that you and your company provide.

- **Choose words effectively** Your use of clear words and phrases will help customers and clients understand your message. Respectful words and phrases can also help you deal with complaints and other sensitive issues.

- **Include basic letter parts** Using formal business letters to communicate with customers and clients conveys respect and professionalism. This can help ensure a good working relationship.

Knowing how to write professionally to customers and clients can increase your value as an employee. Employers want workers who can represent the company well.

Remember!

Most written communications nowadays exist indefinitely in one form or another. So always assume that people beyond your intended audience will be able to read what you write, both now and in the future. Because of this, always choose your words wisely.

Lesson 11 ▪ ▪ ▪
Informing Customers and Clients

Many jobs require employees to communicate with customers in writing. When you write to customers and clients, you need to express yourself clearly. You must also consider which details to include and which to leave out. Perhaps most importantly, you need to choose a format that will ensure that your customers get the message.

Skill Examples

Notifying Customers about Improvements in Service Milo is the store manager for a dry cleaner. The owner, Jim, asks Milo to create two examples for letting customers know about new services the company will be adding. Milo's first example is a notice to be handed out with every customer receipt. His second example is a large notice to be placed in the store's window.

Read each example. Then answer the questions that follow.

EXAMPLE 1

> ### NEW SERVICES AT BRITE-WASH!!
>
> Brite-Wash will be adding NEW service's! In addition to cleaning shirts, sweaters, pants, and coats, we will be providing dry cleaning for other items! These include formal wear, such as wedding dresses, evening gown's, and tuxedos. We will also be able to clean household items, such as area rugs, sleeping bags, and quilts. Ask our owner, Jim MacIntyre, about discount options for bulk orders! Come to Brite-Wash for all your dry cleaning needs!!

1. What information is not clear from this notice?
   A. the store owner's name
   B. whether the store cleans coats and sweaters
   C. the person to contact about bulk orders
   D. the date when the new services will become available
   E. examples of household items they will clean

2. Milo uses a lot of exclamation points. How do they affect his message?
   F. They help readers understand the details.
   G. They make the message clearer.
   H. They make the message dull and sad.
   J. They help organize the message.
   K. They make the most important points difficult to identify.

EXAMPLE 2

NEW SERVICES AT BRITE-WASH!

Starting on April 1, Brite-Wash will expand its dry cleaning capabilities! We will provide full dry cleaning services for the following items:

Formal Wear
Wedding dresses
Evening gowns
Tuxedos
Lamé fabrics
Sequined fabrics

Household Items
Area rugs
Sleeping bags
Quilts (manufactured or
      handmade)
Blankets

Ask our owner, Jim MacIntyre, about discount options for bulk orders.
Come to Brite-Wash for all your dry cleaning needs.

3. Which question cannot be answered based on this notice?

  A. Can the store dry clean handmade quilts?

  B. How much of a discount is given for bulk orders?

  C. When will Brite-Wash begin its new dry cleaning services?

  D. What types of formal wear can be dry cleaned at the store?

  E. Who can provide information about discounts for bulk orders?

4. If a customer scanned this notice, reading only the two headings in bold type, what might he or she learn?

  F. Brite-Wash will provide new services for Jim MacIntyre.

  G. Brite-Wash will provide discounts to customers who place bulk orders.

  H. Brite-Wash will provide dry cleaning for formal wear and household items.

  J. Brite-Wash will clean lamé and sequined fabrics.

  K. Brite-Wash's prices will be reduced.

Think About It Which example communicates information to customers more effectively? In forming your answer, think about the following questions:

- **Format** Which notice will reach a wider notice? Why?

- **Details** How do the examples differ from each other in terms of their details?

Try It Out!

Notifying Customers about Increased Delivery Charges Tamara is a shipping and receiving clerk for a delivery company. Her supervisor sent her this e-mail.

E-mail Message
To: Tamara
Subject: Increase in Shipping Rates

Tamara,

Due to rising fuel costs, we will need to increase our shipping rates. We have decided to increase rates by 3%. This applies to all deliveries, effective May 1. I would like you to write a notice explaining this change to customers. Please include the following details:

- the amount of the increase (we will provide customers with a chart listing all new rates before they go into effect)
- the reason we are making this change
- when the increase will go into effect

Thank you.

Tamara needs to consider the details her supervisor asked her to include in her notice. She also needs to think about the purpose of the notice and how to share it with her audience. She uses the *Pre-Writing Plan* to help her.

Pre-Writing Plan			
TOPIC	**PURPOSE**	**AUDIENCE**	**FORMAT**
Shipping rate increase	To inform clients about the change	Customers who receive deliveries	Notice

Tamara knows that she must present not only the change but also the underlying reason for it. This will help customers understand the reason for the increase. She decides to enclose the notice with each customer's next shipment.

> ### TO OUR VALUED CUSTOMERS
>
> Digby Delivery takes pride in providing speedy service at affordable prices. As a result of rising fuel costs, we have been forced to raise our shipping rates.
>
> Please review this information carefully:
>
> - **All shipping rates will increase by 3%.** For example, if you typically pay $100/month in shipping costs, you can expect to pay $103/month. (We will provide all customers with a chart listing our new rates in detail.)
> - **New shipping rates will go into effect on May 1.**
>
> We apologize for any inconvenience. Thank you for your business.

Remember!

Transition Words Use transition words in your writing to help your audience understand how ideas are connected. Tamara uses a transitional phrase to show a cause-and-effect relationship. She explains that the change is occurring *as a result of* increased fuel costs. She also uses the transitional phrase *for example* to give a specific detail to illustrate a point.

The first line of the message not only identifies the **audience** but also addresses the audience with respect.

The message provides the most important **details** about the change and the reason for it.

Notifying Customers about Increased Delivery Charges Joey is a host at a pizzeria. His manager asks him to post a notice in the restaurant's window informing customers about an increase in prices.

Joey considers the *Pre-Writing Plan* and then writes the notice.

ATTENTION, CUSTOMERS

As you know, fuel costs have been on the rise lately. When fuel costs go up, it has an affect on operating costs. Our ingredients now cost a lot more, and the gas cost for delivering pizza has nearly doubled. Unfortunately, this has effected our business at Paulie's Pizzeria.

As a result, we will have to raise our prices soon.

- The small pizza will cost 50 cents more.
- The large pizza will cost $1.00 more.
- The charge for delivery will be going up a little.

We will continue to use the highest quality ingredients. You deserve the best.

Write a short response to each item below.

1. What details could be added to make the notice clearer?

2. Combine the final two sentences to make the message clearer.

Reflect In these two examples, each writer used the *Pre-Writing Plan* to identify a purpose for writing and choose an appropriate way to share the information. Each writer also made choices about which details to include and which to leave out. Does each writer's choice of details make sense? Is each writer's message clear?

On Your Own ▪ ■ ▪

Read the following scenarios. Then write your own notices based on each scenario.

SCENARIO A Informing Customers about a Change of Address

You manage a bakery that will soon be moving to a new location. The bakery owner asks you to create a notice about the move to send to neighborhood residents. Here is the e-mail the bakery owner sent you.

To:	Manager
Subject:	Upcoming Move

I am very excited about our upcoming move to York Road. We will be able to seat and serve more customers in the larger space. Even better, the new kitchen will help us be more efficient and bake greater quantities.

Please create a notice about the move that can be mailed to the neighborhood residents. Be sure to include the following details:

- The new location is 516 York Road, next to the pet shop. This is just a few blocks away from our current location.
- Customers can park in the lot behind the bakery. The lot entrance is on State Road.
- Our Grand Opening at the new location is scheduled for April 17.
- Customers who arrive between 7:00 A.M. and 11:00 A.M. on that day will receive a free coffee with any order.

Thank you!

Complete the *Pre-Writing Plan* below. Then write the notice.

Pre-Writing Plan			
TOPIC	**PURPOSE**	**AUDIENCE**	**FORMAT**
Change of location		Neighborhood residents	

SCENARIO B Notifying Customers about New Billing and Payment Rules

As an administrative assistant for an office supply company, you frequently communicate with customers. Your supervisor asks you to write to customers and inform them about a new policy. As of next month, all payments must be received within 45 days of delivery. If payments are not received on time, further deliveries and services will be withheld until payment is received.

Complete a *Pre-Writing Plan* on your own. Choose an appropriate format and decide what details to include. Then write the message.

SCENARIO C Notifying Clients about New Business Hours

You work as a veterinarian's assistant. Your office will be expanding its business hours to accommodate more clients. Currently, the office is open from 8:30 A.M. to 5:30 P.M., Monday through Friday. In two weeks, the office will remain open until 7:30 P.M. on Tuesdays, Wednesdays, and Thursdays. It will also be open from 8:30 A.M. to 12:30 P.M. on Saturdays. You have been asked to write a message that will be mailed to clients.

Complete a *Pre-Writing Plan* on your own. Then write the message.

SCENARIO D Notifying Clients about Retirement

As a dispensing optician at an optometrists' office, your primary job is to help patients select eyewear. However, this week you are also helping out with some administrative work while the office manager is on vacation. One of the optometrists, Dr. Garcia, calls you. She would like you to write her patients to let them know about her retirement.

> *DR. GARCIA: Hi, it's Maria Garcia. I need to send out a message to all my current patients. Would you write a draft for me?*
> *YOU: Certainly. What is this message regarding?*
> *DR. GARCIA: Well, I'll be retiring next summer—on June 30, to be exact. I know that's not for a while, but I'd like to let my patients know in advance.*
> *YOU: Okay. What other information should I include?*
> *DR. GARCIA: Please tell my patients that we value their relationship with Clear Sight Vision. Also, let them know that I highly recommend that they stay on as patients of Dr. Jonathon Leibowitz. Be sure to mention that Dr. Leibowitz has fifteen years of experience. If patients want to continue under his care, they don't need to do anything. However, if they want to see a different doctor, they should contact the office as soon as possible.*
> *YOU: I'll take care of that right away.*

Complete a *Pre-Writing Plan* on your own. Then write the draft.

Summary ▪ ▪ ▪

When you write notices, always keep your audience in mind. Additionally, consider these points:

- **Format** Choose a format that will get your audience's attention—for example, a large notice for display, a smaller notice to be handed out, or a letter.

- **Details** Choose your details wisely. Include only the most important information. If a message has too much information, people may ignore it.

- **Clarity** Remember that when you write to customers, you need to present information clearly. Unclear statements can result in a loss of business.

Answers begin on page 144.

Lesson 12 ■ ■ ■
Handling Customer Complaints

For some jobs, communicating with customers involves responding to their complaints. When you respond to customer complaints, it is important to include details and to have a polite and professional tone. You need to acknowledge the problem and provide an indication of how it will be resolved. Your response must present this information clearly.

Skill Examples

Acknowledging Receipt of a Complaint Oliver works as a distribution clerk for a product distribution company. He must respond to a customer's e-mail about a damaged shipment. The following examples show how Oliver might do this.

Read each example. Then answer the questions that follow.

EXAMPLE 1

E-mail Message
To: Arlene Green
Subject: Damaged electronics shipment

Dear Ms. Green,

We received your complaint about the shipment delivered from our warehouse to EZ Electronics store on March 9. You mentioned that one of the boxes were damp, and the MP3 players and such were malfunctioning. Most likely, the goods were left out in the rain or something. Anyway, thanks a million for writing to give us a heads-up on this.

Oliver Smith
Clerk, Distribution Department
Pratt Product Distribution Company
(908) 555-0135, x643

1. Which question cannot be answered based on Oliver's response?

   A. How were the customer's purchases probably damaged?

   B. On what date were the damaged goods shipped?

   C. What number can the customer call to reach Oliver?

   D. What is a possible cause of the damage to the shipment?

   E. Will Pratt Product Distribution Company investigate the complaint?

2. Which word best describes the tone of Oliver's closing sentence?

   F. informal

   G. professional

   H. concerned

   J. annoyed

   K. apologetic

EXAMPLE 2

> **E-mail Message**
>
> **To:** Arlene Green
>
> **Subject:** Damaged electronics shipment
>
> Dear Ms. Green:
>
> Thank you for writing to us about the damaged electronics shipment delivered to EZ Electronics. You noted that the boxes containing MP3 players and smartphones were damp. You also stated that these products were malfunctioning. It is possible that they were exposed to rain.
>
> I have forwarded your message to our Distribution Manager, Al Smith. He will work with the warehouse and delivery teams to determine how this problem occurred. Mr. Smith will also contact you soon to discuss resolving this issue.
>
> Please except our apologies for any inconvenience.
>
> Sincerely,
>
> Oliver Smith
> Clerk, Distribution Department
> Pratt Product Distribution Company
> (908) 555-0135, x643

Remember!

Word Choice When writing, people often confuse the words *except* and *accept* because they sound so similar. In the last sentence of *Example 2*, Oliver incorrectly writes *except* instead of *accept*. An electronic spell-check program would not find this mistake. Remember to check your writing to make sure that you have used words correctly.

3. What information is not clear from Oliver's e-mail?

   A. the types of products that were damaged

   B. the position Oliver holds at his company

   C. the name of the distribution manager

   D. how the company will begin to investigate the problem

   E. when the customer can expect to hear from the company again

4. What other detail would be appropriate to include in this e-mail?

   F. contact information for all the senior managers at the company

   G. a comment about how often such damage occurs

   H. the names of the warehouse clerks and drivers

   J. testimonials from other customers about how quickly the company resolves complaints

   K. the date the shipment was delivered

Think About It Which example is more effective in acknowledging the complaint? In forming your answer, think about the following questions.

- **Details** What details should be included to show that the company understands the problem and is working to address it?

- **Clarity** Why is it important to use specific words rather than unclear words when discussing a customer's problem?

Try It Out!

Responding to Complaints As a quality assurance associate for a frozen food company, Carol responds to complaints. She receives the following e-mail.

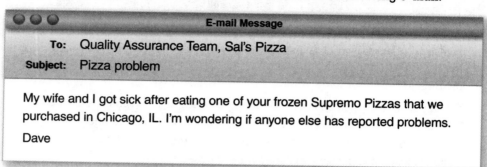

E-mail Message

To: Quality Assurance Team, Sal's Pizza

Subject: Pizza problem

My wife and I got sick after eating one of your frozen Supremo Pizzas that we purchased in Chicago, IL. I'm wondering if anyone else has reported problems.

Dave

Carol wants to apologize to the customer, investigate the problem, and resolve it. However, she must obtain more information first. Carol must include relevant questions in her response. She uses the *Pre-Writing Plan* to help her.

Pre-Writing Plan			
TOPIC	PURPOSE	AUDIENCE	FORMAT
Customer illness following product consumption	To apologize and obtain information about the problem	Customer	E-mail

Carol decides to include an apology as well as a list of information that she will need from the customer in order to investigate the problem.

E-mail Message

To: Dave

Subject: Re: Pizza problem

Dear Dave:

I am very sorry to learn of your recent illness and would like to obtain more information so that we can resolve the problem quickly. I would like to speak with you about this matter.

Please review the following list before we talk. Be prepared to provide as much of this information as possible. This will help us address the problem.

Purchase Information

- Store name and location (including street name)
- Type of pizza purchased (size and style)
- Date of purchase
- Code located in white "Enjoy By" box on the side panel (if available), *or*
- Code located on shrink wrap on bottom of pizza (if available)

Thank you for contacting us. On behalf of Sal's Pizza, I apologize for any inconvenience this problem has caused you.

Carol Chen, Sal's Frozen Pizza
1-800-555-0126, x 267

Responding to Complaints Terrell manages a cleaning service. He must respond to a customer who sent an e-mail complaining that his kitchen had not been cleaned properly.

Terrell considers the *Pre-Writing Plan* and then writes the response.

To: Steve
Subject: Re: Kitchen cleaning

Dear Steve:

I'm sorry to hear you were not satisfied with how our cleaning staff cleaned your kitchen and stuff. What can I say? These things happen occasionally. Our team is responsible for cleaning many houses every day. You can't blame them if sometimes they slack off a little.

Please send me more details about the problem. This will help me make sure it does not happen again. Thanks. Again, I apologize this is just how it goes sometimes. We will make it up to you.

Sincerely,

Terrell Darcy, Manager
Sparkle Cleaning Services

Remember!

Run-on Sentence
Sometimes a run-on sentence is a result of combining two sentences without using a conjunction. Terrell's second from last sentence is a run-on. It can be corrected by breaking it apart, like this: *Again, I apologize. This is just how it goes sometimes.* Alternatively, it can be combined properly like this: *Again, I apologize, but this is just how it goes sometimes.*

Write a short response to each item below.

1. Which words and phrases are too informal for a business communication?

2. The last sentence of Terrell's e-mail does not explain how Terrell might try to make up for the company's poor service. Rewrite the sentence to make it clearer.

Reflect In these two examples, the writers used the *Pre-Writing Plan* to determine their purposes for writing. They also had to choose which details to include and how to state their messages clearly. Is each message clear and detailed enough to fulfill each writer's purpose? Is the tone of each message professional?

On Your Own ▪ ▪ ▪

Read the following scenarios. Then write your own communications based on each scenario.

SCENARIO A Responding to a Complaint

You work as a technician at an appliance store. Recently, you received the following e-mail from a customer whose refrigerator was repaired at your store.

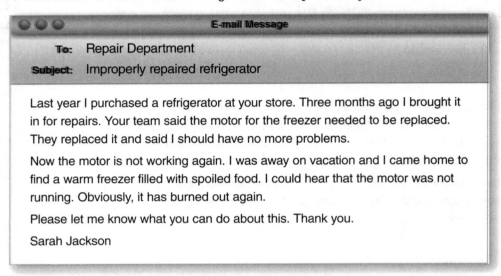

E-mail Message

To: Repair Department

Subject: Improperly repaired refrigerator

Last year I purchased a refrigerator at your store. Three months ago I brought it in for repairs. Your team said the motor for the freezer needed to be replaced. They replaced it and said I should have no more problems.

Now the motor is not working again. I was away on vacation and I came home to find a warm freezer filled with spoiled food. I could hear that the motor was not running. Obviously, it has burned out again.

Please let me know what you can do about this. Thank you.

Sarah Jackson

Complete the *Pre-Writing Plan* below. Then write the e-mail.

Pre-Writing Plan			
TOPIC	PURPOSE	AUDIENCE	FORMAT
Burned out replacement freezer motor			E-mail

SCENARIO B Recording Complaints

As a customer service representative for an online clothing store, you receive a complaint through e-mail. The customer states that a suit jacket he ordered has a tear in the sleeve. The customer wants to return the item. However, because it was on clearance when he ordered it, the suit jacket cannot be returned.

You would like to help the customer. To do so, you need to know the customer's contact information, the specific item purchased, the date of the purchase, and the order number on the customer's receipt. Once you have this information, you will forward the complaint to the customer service manager. The manager will decide how to handle the situation.

Complete a *Pre-Writing Plan* on your own. Determine your purpose and what details you must include to make sure your message is clear. Then write the response e-mail.

SCENARIO C Acknowledging Receipt of a Complaint

You work as an administrative assistant for a cable company. A customer contacts you with a complaint. He says that a technician was scheduled to install cable at his house between 10:00 A.M. and 2:00 P.M. on Saturday. However, the technician never arrived. You must inform the customer that you received his complaint. You must also let him know that the company will contact him within forty-eight hours to reschedule the installation.

Complete a *Pre-Writing Plan* on your own. Then write the response.

SCENARIO D Responding to a Complaint

You are a carpenter with your own carpentry business. A customer leaves you the following voice-mail message.

> *Hi, this is Lara Coretti. I'm calling about the kitchen cabinets you installed yesterday. I think one of these cabinets was damaged during the installation. There is a small scratch near the bottom of the cabinet door. Also, the hinge is sticking. The cabinet door still opens, but not as easily as the other cabinet doors. Please let me know when you can come out to look at it. Thank you.*

You believe the scratch was your fault, but the sticky hinge is probably a manufacturing defect. You can fix the scratch and will do so for free. You can replace the hinge easily if the customer orders a new one from the manufacturer.

Complete a *Pre-Writing Plan* on your own. Then write the response.

Summary ▪ ▪ ▪

When you respond to a customer's complaint, first determine your purpose. Make sure the details are clear to your reader. Additionally, keep these points in mind:

- **Details** Restate the key details the customer provided about the problem. Include specific details about how the company will follow up.

- **Clarity** To ensure that your message is clear, address items specifically rather than generally. You should also proofread your response to prevent errors from causing confusion.

- **Tone** When you respond to a customer's complaint, make sure that your tone is polite and professional. This will help reassure your customer that you take the complaint seriously.

Answers begin on page 144.

Lesson 13 ▪ ▪ ▪
Expressing Gratitude

Some jobs require you to express gratitude to customers or clients in writing. When you express gratitude, you should strive for a warm but professional tone. You also need to determine an appropriate format for your message and to focus on expressing your thoughts clearly.

Skill Examples

Writing a Thank You Note Paula is a salesperson for a medical supply company. She has just met with staff members at a local hospital and is hoping to become one of their suppliers. Paula wants to write to thank the hospital staff for meeting with her. The following examples show how Paula might do this.

Read each example. Then answer the questions that follow.

EXAMPLE 1

KRAGER MEDICAL SUPPLY　　　1207 Pinebrook Lane　　Chicago, IL 60601

April 1, 2011

Stacey Chambers, M.D. and Felicia Stone, R.N.
Cedar View Hospital, Suite 100
800 Woodland Drive
Chicago, IL 60606

Dear Dr. Chambers and Nurse Stone:

Thank you for making the time to meat with me today.

I will be sending you a catalog of our supplies soon. Please let us know witch supplies you are interested in. I look forward to hearing from you.

Thank you.

---

1. Which of the following questions can readers answer using Paula's letter?
   A. Who did Paula meet at the hospital?
   B. What specific topics were discussed during Paula's meeting?
   C. What are some of the specialty items Krager supplies?
   D. Which items can be purchased at a discount in bulk?
   E. What is a common challenge faced by hospital staff?

2. What other information would be appropriate to include in this letter?
   F. Paula's phone number and e-mail address
   G. the hospital's phone number
   H. the names of all the sales associates at Krager
   J. a list of all the hospitals near Cedar View Hospital
   K. a catalog of medical supplies offered by Krager's competitor

EXAMPLE 2

KRAGER MEDICAL SUPPLY   1207 Pinebrook Lane   Chicago, IL 60601

April 1, 2011

Stacey Chambers, M.D. and Felicia Stone, R.N.
Cedar View Hospital, Suite 100
800 Woodland Drive
Chicago, IL 60606

Dear Dr. Chambers and Nurse Stone:

Thank you both for taking the time to meet with me today. I appreciated the chance to talk with you about Krager Medical Supply's products and prices. In particular, I was interested to learn that you will be building a new wing for your maternity ward. As we discussed, Krager can offer significant discounts on bulk orders of standard supplies, such as hospital beds and food service carts.

Please contact me at 201-555-0189 if you are interested in using us as one of your suppliers. I hope to hear from you soon. Thank you.

Sincerely,

Paula Danielson

Paula Danielson, Sales Associate

Remember!

Letter Parts When you send a letter to a customer, always include the basic parts of a letter: the heading, greeting, body paragraphs, closing, and signature. In *Example 2*, Paula includes all these letter parts, which make her note complete and professional.

3. What question cannot be answered based on Paula's thank you letter?
   A. When did Paula meet Dr. Chambers and Nurse Stone?
   B. How can the recipient contact Paula?
   C. How much of a discount does Krager offer on bulk purchases?
   D. Why did Paula meet with Dr. Chambers and Nurse Stone?
   E. What is one way Paula's company can meet the hospital's specific needs?

4. What other document would be appropriate to include with this letter?
   F. business cards from all of the sales associates at Krager
   G. a copy of Paula's university degree
   H. a list of other area hospitals that work with Krager
   J. a catalog of supplies provided by Krager Medical Supply
   K. an explanation of why competitors' products are inferior

Think About It Which example do you think is more effective? In forming your answer, think about the following questions.

- **Tone** What tone or attitude should you try to convey when writing a thank you note to a client or customer?

- **Clarity** How can your choice of language and details affect the clarity of your thank you letter?

Try It Out!

Thanking a Client for a Referral Miguel works as an independent handyman who performs small home repair and improvement jobs. A former client sent Miguel the following letter to let him know she referred him to a friend.

June 30, 2011

Hi, Miguel,

Thanks so much for the great job you did painting the bedrooms and fixing that broken-down fence in our backyard. I also really appreciated your assistance in retiling the kitchen. I couldn't have gotten all of this done without you!

I wanted to let you know that I've recommended you to a friend of mine who just moved into the neighborhood. She bought a large, older home that needs a lot of fixing up. I am sure you will be hearing from her soon.

Thanks again–

Marta Anderson

Miguel wants to thank the client. He needs to express his gratitude clearly and with the appropriate tone. He also must choose a format for his message. He uses the *Pre-Writing Plan* to help him.

Pre-Writing Plan			
TOPIC	**PURPOSE**	**AUDIENCE**	**FORMAT**
A referral	To thank customer for a referral	Ms. Anderson	Thank you note

Miguel chooses to use the same format as his customer used: a brief note. However, he decides to use a slightly more formal tone and to type his note.

MIGUEL SANCHEZ
132 Maple Lane   Warrenville, MI 60342

July 6, 2011

Dear Ms. Anderson,

I am so glad to know that you were pleased with the work I did on your house. You have a beautiful home, and it was a pleasure to work on it.

I also want to thank you for the referral. In my line of work, people build their businesses slowly through word-of-mouth. A personal recommendation makes a big difference. I greatly appreciate your taking the time to recommend me.

I look forward to having the opportunity to work with your friend.

Best wishes,

Miguel Sanchez

Miguel Sanchez

Remember!

Pronoun-Antecedent Agreement When you write a letter, make sure that your pronouns agree with their antecedents. In the second sentence of his letter, Miguel tells Ms. Anderson that she has "a beautiful home and it was a pleasure to work on it." The pronoun—the second *it* in the sentence—refers to the antecedent *house*. Both *home* and *it* are singular.

The note accomplishes Miguel's **purpose** of expressing his thanks.

The **format** Miguel chose is suitable for this context.

Acknowledging a Customer's Appreciation Cherie works as a flight attendant. She has learned that a customer who frequently flies with her has e-mailed the airline praising her customer service skills. Cherie wants to write an e-mail to thank him.

Cherie considers the *Pre-Writing Plan* and then writes the e-mail.

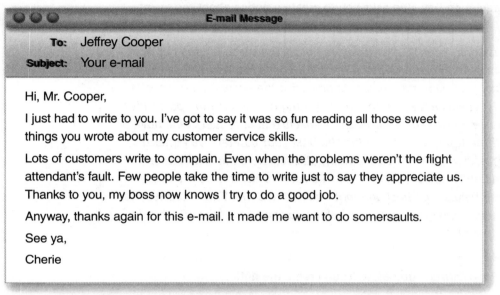

E-mail Message

To: Jeffrey Cooper

Subject: Your e-mail

Hi, Mr. Cooper,

I just had to write to you. I've got to say it was so fun reading all those sweet things you wrote about my customer service skills.

Lots of customers write to complain. Even when the problems weren't the flight attendant's fault. Few people take the time to write just to say they appreciate us. Thanks to you, my boss now knows I try to do a good job.

Anyway, thanks again for this e-mail. It made me want to do somersaults.

See ya,

Cherie

Write a short response to each item below.

1. The first sentence is not clear. The reader does not know why the writer is writing to him. What detail could be added to make the purpose of the letter clear?

2. The last two sentences and the closing are too informal. Rewrite them to express gratitude while maintaining a professional tone.

Reflect Miguel and Cherie both used the *Pre-Writing Plan* to help them choose a format for their letters. Does each format suit the writer's purpose? Do the writers express themselves clearly, using an appropriate tone? What effect does an overly informal tone have on a reader?

Remember!

Sentence Fragments
Even in a brief note, avoid sentence fragments. A sentence fragment is an incomplete thought. In Cherie's letter, *Even when the problems weren't the flight attendant's fault* is a sentence fragment. One way to fix it is to combine it with the previous sentence: *Lots of customers write to complain, even when the problems weren't the flight attendant's fault.* Sentence fragments can cause confusion and make you appear unprofessional.

On Your Own ▪ ▪ ▪

Read the following scenarios. Then write your own communications based on each scenario.

SCENARIO A Showing Appreciation of Customers

You are studying to become a massage therapist. To support yourself, you work as a receptionist at a day spa. The owner leaves you a voice mail about the upcoming Customer Appreciation Day. She asks you to create a notice about the event.

> *Hello, this is Lena. I don't know if you've heard, but we're having our first ever Customer Appreciation Day on April 30. That's just two weeks from today. I'd like you to create a poster to advertise the event on our website. Be sure to let customers know that if they bring a friend to our spa on that day, both will receive a free manicure. Also, current customers who have visited us three times or more within the past year can receive either a facial or a pedicure at half-price. Finally, all customers that come in on that day will automatically be entered in a raffle. They'll have the chance to win a free Deluxe Spa Package that's valued at $300. This is our way of saying thanks to everyone who has helped our business take off. Thanks for your help with this.*

Complete the *Pre-Writing Plan* below. Then create the notice.

Pre-Writing Plan			
TOPIC	PURPOSE	AUDIENCE	FORMAT
Customer Appreciation Day			Notice

SCENARIO B Writing a Recommendation

In your job as an electrician, you recently completed all of the wiring for a restaurant. Your supervisor had sent an apprentice, Seantrell, to help you. Although Seantrell was new to the job, you found him to be more knowledgeable than most beginners. He was also very helpful and had a great attitude. In fact, he even worked through some of his scheduled breaks so the job would be completed on time. You would like to write a letter to your supervisor praising Seantrell's skill and attitude and recommending that he be given more work.

Complete a *Pre-Writing Plan* on your own. Decide how to state your ideas clearly and what tone to use. Then write the recommendation letter.

SCENARIO C Creating a Postcard to Show Appreciation

You work as a graphic designer for the public relations department of a community college. Recently, the college held an open house. Your supervisor asks you to create a postcard to send to all the people who attended. The card should thank them for their interest in the college and for coming to the open house. He also wants you to include information about where prospective students can access application forms and the date by which they must submit applications for the next semester.

Complete a *Pre-Writing Plan* on your own. Then create the postcard.

SCENARIO D Creating a Personal Thank You Card

As a nursing-home aide, you often get to know residents and their families very well. Recently, one of the residents, Mrs. Smith, left the home because her family was moving to another state. As a token of appreciation, the family sent you the following note and a gift. You want to send them a thank you card in response.

> May 4, 2011
>
> We really appreciate all you did for our mother, Adele Smith. We know that with Mom's very limited mobility, it can be difficult to provide the round-the-clock care she needs. Thank you for always being dependable and treating Mom with kindness and respect. It meant so much to her and to us.
>
> Mom has often mentioned your interest in art, so we have enclosed a six-month membership to the Urban Art Museum. Please accept this small token of our appreciation. Thanks again for everything.
>
> The Smith Family

Complete a *Pre-Writing Plan* on your own. Then create the thank you card.

Summary ▪ ▪ ▪

When you write to express gratitude, choose an appropriate format, state your ideas clearly, and use an appropriate tone. Keep these points in mind:

- **Tone** A warm, friendly tone is appropriate when you express gratitude. However, take care not to use an overly informal tone, which can make you appear unprofessional.

- **Format** Depending on the situation, you might express gratitude in a business letter, a brief note, an e-mail, or in another format.

- **Clarity** To ensure that your message is clear, be specific about why you are grateful.

Answers begin on page 145.

Lesson 14 ■ ■ ■
Requesting Payment

Employees in many different industries sometimes have to request payment from customers or clients. When you write to request payment, you must include relevant details and present them in an organized way. You must also use a respectful and professional tone.

Skill Examples

Sending an Invoice Rose works for a catering business. Her manager asks her to send an invoice for a wedding they catered the previous week. The following examples show how Rose might do this.

Read each example. Then answer the questions that follow.

EXAMPLE 1

BILLING DATE: June 9, 2011

INSTRUCTIONS: Review the invoice carefully. If there are ANY mistakes or discrepancies, contact Griswell Catering IMMEDIATELY. Do NOT submit any form of payment not on the list. This will DELAY the processing of your payment. Remit payment within 60 days of the billing date; All checks MUST be made to Griswell Catering Company.

INVOICE

Invoice Number	Customer	Griswell Catering Contact
WED060611	Hernandez, Joseph	510-555-0167 x4567
Products and Services		
Appetizer Trays; Dinners—chicken; Dinners—seafood; Beverage stations; Wait staff hours		

TOTAL:　　　　$2880.00

1. Which question cannot be answered based on this communication?
   A. When is the payment for this invoice due?
   B. To whom should the check be made out?
   C. What types of dinners were served at the Hernandez wedding?
   D. How much did each of the different products and services cost?
   E. What number should Mr. Hernandez call if he has questions?

2. Which word best describes the tone of the instructions of this invoice?
   F. pleasant
   G. excited
   H. vague
   J. informal
   K. unfriendly

EXAMPLE 2

BILLING DATE: June 9, 2011

Please review the instructions below before sending payment. Thank you for choosing Griswell Catering Company to cater your special event!

INSTRUCTIONS: First review the invoice thoroughly. If there are any mistakes or discrepancies, please contact Rose Henderson at Griswell Catering immediately. Next, decide whether you will pay by major credit card or check. All checks should be made out to Griswell Catering Company. Finally, please send payment within 60 days of the billing date.

INVOICE

Invoice Number	Customer	Griswell Catering Contact	
WED060611	Hernandez, Joseph	Rose Henderson, 510-555-0167 x4567	

Products and Services

Quantity	Description	Unit Price	Extended Price
10	Appetizer Trays	$40.00	$400.00
50	Dinners—chicken	$20.00	$1000.00
50	Dinners—seafood	$20.00	$1000.00
3	Beverage stations	$100.00	$300.00
15	Wait staff hours	$12.00	$180.00
		TOTAL	**$2880.00**

3. What information is not clear from the invoice?

   A. how many beverage stations the catering company set up

   B. whom Mr. Hernandez can contact if he has questions

   C. what kinds of appetizers were included on the appetizer trays

   D. how much the catering company charged for seafood dinners

   E. who the checks should be made out to

4. What information would be most useful to add to these instructions?

   F. the contact details of the customer

   G. the address where the event took place

   H. the procedure to follow if payment is made by credit card

   J. additional charges if payment is not made on time

   K. the name of the bank where the check will be deposited

Think About It Which example communicates relevant billing information more effectively? In forming your answer, think about the following questions.

- **Details** What kinds of details should be included on an invoice to ensure that the customer understands it?

- **Tone** What tone is appropriate for an invoice? How can you ensure that your tone leaves a positive impression?

Try It Out!

Sending a Payment Reminder Joe works as a personal trainer and keeps track of client payments in a ledger. He must send a reminder to a client who is late with some payments.

PAYMENT LEDGER—APRIL 2011

Invoice Number	Client	Services	Invoice Total	Date billed	Payment received
04002	Sorrentino	Strength training	$50	4/22/11	5/1/11
04003	Johnson	Baseline fitness	$30	4/13/11	–
04004	Johnson	Strength training	$50	4/15/11	–

Joe must decide which details to include in the reminder. He also needs to strike the right tone—firm but professional. Joe uses the *Pre-Writing Plan* to help him.

Pre-Writing Plan			
TOPIC	PURPOSE	AUDIENCE	FORMAT
Overdue payment	To remind customer of payment	Mr. Johnson, client	Business letter

Joe thinks it would be helpful to include an itemized list of charges. He also decides to remind the client of his policy concerning late payments.

JOE SILVERMAN   P.O. Box 3901   Haightsboro, NJ 08666

May 5, 2011

Mr. Timothy Johnson
29 Green Valley Lane
Haightsboro, NJ 08666

Dear Mr. Johnson:

▶This is a friendly reminder that your payments totaling $80 are overdue. As we discussed in our first meeting, payment for any services rendered must be received within fourteen (14) days. Failure to pay within twenty-one (21) days will result in training sessions being discontinued.

Please review the list of charges below and send payment as soon as possible.
* **Service:** Baseline fitness assessment ($30); **Payment due:** 4/27/11
* **Service:** Strength training session ($50); **Payment due:** 4/29/11

If this list is in error, or if you have already sent your payment, please contact me at 732-555-0190. Thank you.

Sincerely,

Joe Silverman

Remember!

Clarity To ensure that your message is clear, include the amount due, the actions the customer should take, and any relevant business policies. Joe states this information clearly in the first paragraph of his reminder letter.

The **purpose** of the letter is stated clearly in the first sentence.

A business letter is an appropriately formal **format** for late-payment requests.

Writing a Form Cover Letter Jolie works as a legal assistant for a private tax attorney. The attorney asks her to write a form cover letter to accompany the itemized bill that will be sent to clients.

Jolie considers the *Pre-Writing Plan* and then writes the letter.

SMITH TAX LAW
4127 Monterrey Avenue   Granville, IA 50999

April 1, 2011

[Client Address]

Dear [Client Name]:

You know, your payment of _____ is overdue. We are sure this is just an oversight. However, please make sure to send your payment as soon as possible.

Let me know if the itemized bill contains any mistakes. I can be reached at 302-555-0111. Please look over all of the charges in the attached itemized bill.

Thank you.

Sincerely,

Jolie Carter
Legal Assistant

Write a short response to each item below.

1. Which sentence in the final paragraph should appear at the beginning of that paragraph?

2. The first sentence uses an overly informal tone. Rewrite this sentence to sound more businesslike.

Reflect Joe and Jolie both used the *Pre-Writing Plan* to determine which details to include. They also decided how to organize their letters and what tone to use. Does each letter have helpful details and an appropriate tone? Does the organization of each letter help make the information clear to the reader?

On Your Own ▪ ▪ ▪

Read the following scenarios. Then write a letter for each scenario.

SCENARIO A Writing a Request for Payment

You are a wedding photographer. You must send a customer the following notice of payment for recently delivered photos. You will enclose a letter with the notice. Your letter will explain that the payment is due in thirty days and that you accept only checks or money orders.

NOTICE OF PAYMENT DUE

Jack and Yolanda Michaels
92 Magnolia Lane
Carterville, PA 19888
Payment Due **$1484.00**

Item	Quantity	Cost per Unit	Total
16" x 20" wedding portrait	1	$150	$150
large wedding album	1	$500	$500
small wedding album	2	$300	$600
family photo package (mixed sizes)	1	$150	$150
		SUBTOTAL	$1400
		SALES TAX	$84
		TOTAL	$1484

Complete the *Pre-Writing Plan* below. Then write the letter.

Pre-Writing Plan			
TOPIC	PURPOSE	AUDIENCE	FORMAT
Request for payment			Business letter

SCENARIO B Writing a Payment Reminder

You are a self-employed nanny. Recently, you received a check from a client for the previous month's work. However, the amount of the check was less than what you were owed. You charge $10 per hour for your services. You worked a total of 166 hours—four 40-hour weeks, plus one weekend when you worked 16 hours. You should have received $1760, but you received only $1600. Since you do not work weekends regularly, you believe the family just forgot to include the 16 weekend hours. You decide to write a note explaining the issue.

Complete a *Pre-Writing Plan* on your own. Decide which details to include, how to organize them, and what tone you should use. Then write the note.

SCENARIO C Sending a Second Payment Request

You work as an accounts receivable clerk for a brick-paving company. Recently, you invoiced a client for work the company did to create a small paved garden path. The total payment due is $255. This is for 15 hours of work at $17 per hour. Payment was due on April 15, and it is now April 30. You must send the client a payment reminder.

Complete a *Pre-Writing Plan* on your own. Then write the letter.

SCENARIO D Explaining an Invoice

You are a roofer who owns your own business. Recently, you fixed a client's roof. The client calls and leaves you the following message.

> Hi, this is Mr. Harada. I received your invoice and I'm a little confused about what the different charges mean. Could you please clarify how you arrived at the total of $235? Thank you.

Below is the invoice you sent the client. After reviewing the invoice, you decide to send a letter explaining each of the charges listed for both materials and labor.

INVOICE

Item/Service	Cost per Unit/Hour	Item Quantity/ Hours Worked	Total
3-tab Fiberglass Shingles	$50/square	1 roofing square (100 square feet)	$50
#15 lb. Roofing Felt	$25/square	1 roofing square (100 square feet)	$25
Labor	$20/hr	8 hours	$160.00
		TOTAL	**$235.00**

Complete a *Pre-Writing Plan* on your own. Then write the letter.

Summary ▪ ▪ ▪

When you write a request for payment, make sure it is detailed, organized in a way that is easy to understand, and professional in tone. Keep these points in mind:

- **Details** Include a breakdown of specific charges to help the client or customer understand how you calculated the payment total.

- **Organization** Use headings, along with tables or lists, to organize information clearly. For simple requests, paragraphs may provide enough information.

- **Tone** Maintain a neutral, businesslike tone. Payment requests should not be overly warm or informal. However, take care to avoid sounding harsh, even when you are writing about a late payment.

Answers begin on page 146.

Writing to Other Organizations ...

Writing for work often involves communicating with people from other organizations. You may need to write to ask for a price quote or to express a complaint. Perhaps your company is meeting with another company, and you need to send an agenda.

In this section, you will learn the skills needed to communicate effectively when writing to other organizations.

Lesson 15: Requesting Information Asking another organization for information requires a clearly stated and organized purpose. *Tasks include*:

- Requesting Product Information
- Requesting Information about Charges
- Requesting Delivery Information
- Requesting Bids and Quotes

Lesson 16: Offering Feedback Providing positive or negative feedback to another organization requires a clear message, specific details, and a respectful tone. *Tasks include*:

- Suggesting Improvements
- Informing about a Technical Problem
- Writing a Complaint
- Expressing a Compliment

Lesson 17: Requesting Meetings Arranging meetings with other organizations requires specific details regarding the attendees, time, location, purpose, and agenda. *Tasks include*:

- Launching a Project
- Proposing a Joint Project
- Responding to a Meeting Request
- Requesting a Meeting
- Proposing New Agenda Items
- Proposing a New Meeting Time

Lesson 18: Responding to Queries Answering questions from other organizations requires sufficient details and a clear and organized response. *Tasks include*:

- Responding to a Request for Information
- Responding to Payment Queries
- Responding to Queries about Price Changes
- Responding to Queries about Delays

Key Factors for Writing to Other Organizations ▪ ▪ ▪

Many workers have to write to a broad range of organizations. This requires versatility. You need to know your audience and apply an appropriate tone to your message. Regardless of the audience, it is always appropriate to be courteous and professional. To write effectively to other organizations, you must also write clearly, include only the relevant details, and organize your message logically.

In Theme 4, you will also learn to:

- **Use comparative and superlative adjectives** Using correct comparative and superlative adjectives is important for clear communication. It also helps employees at other organizations feel confident in your abilities.

- **Use sequence words** Sequence words identify the order in which events or steps take place. Using sequence words when communicating helps ensure that your message is clear.

- **Include basic letter parts** Your writing is often the first impression you make with another organization. Including basic letter parts in your communications demonstrates professionalism and respect.

By knowing how to effectively write to other organizations, you can demonstrate to your employer that you are responsible and trustworthy.

Remember!
When you write to other organizations, you are representing your company. Even when you are on friendly terms with someone, keep your writing professionally appropriate. Always assume that you may be asked to justify what you write.

Lesson 15 ▪ ▪ ▪
Requesting Information

You may sometimes need to write to other organizations to request information. When doing this, your request must be clearly stated and organized.

Skill Examples

Requesting Product Information Al works as a livestock caretaker on an organic farm. He needs to write to a sales representative about a new brand of feed he is considering buying. The following examples show how Al might do this.

Read each example. Then answer the questions that follow.

EXAMPLE 1

E-mail Message
To: Bill
Subject: Questions about Farm Supply's Livestock Feed

Dear Bill,

It was nice meeting you at the farm last week. I am interested in learning more.

For the cattle feed I would like to know about the crude protein content of your Calf Starter Formula. How does your Calf Starter Formula rate in terms of other vitamins and minerals? What about calcium in your Chick Starter Formula?

For the poultry feed, how much protein and fat are in your formula for chicks? How much can I save if I go with large bags over small bags? What is the cost of each type of cattle feed?

Al Rylant
Livestock Caretaker, Pricerowe Farms

1. How is Al's e-mail organized?
   A. Questions about cattle feed are in the second paragraph, and questions about poultry feed are in the third paragraph.
   B. All the questions about poultry feed are in the second paragraph.
   C. The e-mail first explains what Al's job is at the farm.
   D. Questions about cattle feed and poultry feed are in both the second and third paragraphs.
   E. The e-mail closes by asking a series of questions about cattle feed.

2. What is the effect of the phrase "What about…" in questions like this: "What about calcium in your Chick Starter Formula?"
   F. It improves the overall organization of Al's message.
   G. It makes Al seem friendly and approachable.
   H. It creates a good impression because the question uses correct grammar.
   J. It makes Al's tone sound overly businesslike and not warm enough.
   K. It makes it difficult to know exactly what information Al needs.

Remember!

Punctuation Before sending any work-related correspondence, check your writing to make sure you have used correct punctuation. In the second paragraph of *Example 1,* Al should have placed a comma after the word *feed,* like this: "For the cattle feed, I would like to know about the crude protein content of your Calf Starter Formula." Without the comma, the sentence might initially be read as, "For the cattle feed *that* I would like…." Adding the comma helps avoid confusion.

EXAMPLE 2

```
●●●                    E-mail Message
    To:  Bill
  Subject:  Questions about Farm Supply's Livestock Feed
```

Dear Bill,

Thank you so much for meeting with me at the farm last week. I am interested in learning more about your products. Specifically, I have the following questions.

Cattle Feed
- What is the crude protein content of your Calf Starter Formula?
- What is the percentage of other vitamins and minerals in the formula?
- What is the crude protein content of your Cattle Grower/Finisher Formula?
- What is the cost of each type of cattle feed per 50-lb. bag?

Poultry Feed
- What is the crude protein and fat content of your Chick Starter Formula?
- What is the cost of each type of poultry feed per 15-lb. bag? How much could I save by ordering 25-lb. bags?

This information will help me decide whether to use Farm Supply's products.

Al Rylant

Livestock Caretaker, Pricerowe Farms

Remember!

Details When you are making an important decision, be sure to be specific when requesting the information you need to help you make that decision. Do not assume that the reader knows what you want. In *Example 2,* Al clearly asks several specific questions about nutritional value and pricing.

3. Which question cannot be answered based on Al's e-mail?

   A. Why is Al writing to Bill?

   B. What was the date of Al and Bill's meeting?

   C. What are the two main topics Al wants to know more about?

   D. What does Al want to know about the cost of the company's cattle feed?

   E. What does Al want to know about the content of the poultry feed?

4. Which is not one of the techniques Al uses to organize his e-mail?

   F. charts

   G. headings

   H. bullet points

   J. paragraph breaks

   K. transition words

Think About It Which example is more likely to obtain the information Al wants? In forming your answer, think about the following questions.

- **Organization** Which e-mail is organized more clearly for the reader? How was this accomplished?

- **Clarity** If Al's questions are unclear to the sales representative, what problems could result?

Try It Out!

Requesting Delivery Information Yolanda leads a team of ship loaders. She receives the following voice mail from a shipping company about an upcoming produce delivery.

> *Hi, Yolanda, this is Ed. I wanted to let you know that you can expect a major shipment of fresh produce early next week. Please be sure to assemble a large enough team to handle all the loading and unloading. It's important that we have enough workers present. Thanks a lot.*

Yolanda needs to know how large the shipment is and exactly when to expect it. She decides to respond with an e-mail. She must phrase her questions clearly and organize her response carefully. She uses the *Pre-Writing Plan* to help her.

Pre-Writing Plan

TOPIC	PURPOSE	AUDIENCE	FORMAT
Upcoming produce delivery	To obtain information about size and timing of shipment	Shipping company	E-mail

Yolanda needs all of her questions answered. She uses a bulleted list so that each question stands out.

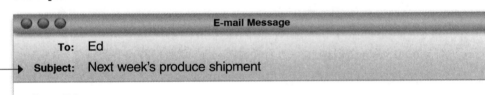

E-mail Message

To: Ed

Subject: Next week's produce shipment

Dear Ed,

Thank you for informing me about next week's produce shipment. To ensure that we are sufficiently prepared for the shipment, I need answers to the following questions:

- On what date can I expect to receive the shipment?
- At approximately what time is this shipment due to arrive? I understand you may not be able to give an exact time, but please provide an estimate.
- How many crates of produce is included in this shipment?

Your answers to these questions will help me make sure we are staffed appropriately for your shipment. I appreciate your help.

Sincerely,
Yolanda

Requesting Delivery Information Kirk is an electrical technician at an office building. He recently placed an online order for some parts for a repair job. After placing the order, Kirk realized that his receipt did not include a date for delivery. Kirk must e-mail the supplier to find out when the parts will arrive.

Kirk considers the *Pre-Writing Plan* and then writes the e-mail.

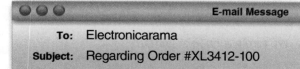

E-mail Message
To: Electronicarama
Subject: Regarding Order #XL3412-100

This e-mail is in reference to an order I just placed online. I need the parts for the Malland Office Building, which was affected by the worse thunderstorm we have had in years. The building's lighting and security systems were badly damaged. I ordered the following parts.

- 3 fluorescent light panels
- 6 LED tube lights with 18-watt Power and 110/220V AC voltage
- 2 Siamese cables for use with a 12V DC security camera

My order receipt did not tell me when the parts would arrive. Please give me an estimated date of delivery for these parts. Thank you.

Sincerely,

Kirk Chapman

Remember!

Comparative and Superlative Adjectives For most adjectives, add *-er* or *-est* to make comparisons. The adjective *bad,* however, is irregular. Use *worse* to compare two people or things and *worst* to compare three or more people or things. In the second sentence of this message, Kirk uses the adjective *worse*. He should have used *worst* because he is comparing many storms.

Write a short response to each item below.

1. What detail from the last paragraph could be moved to the first paragraph to get Kirk's point across more clearly?

2. The first paragraph contains unnecessary details. This makes it difficult to clearly understand the purpose of the message. Rewrite this paragraph without the unnecessary details. You should be able to do this in one or two sentences.

Reflect In the examples on these two pages, the writers used the *Pre-Writing Plan* to decide how to organize their ideas and express them clearly. Did the writers clearly state their main points and organize their writing in a way that makes sense?

On Your Own ▪ ■ ▪

Read the following scenarios. Then write your own communications based on each scenario.

SCENARIO A Requesting Product Information

As a floral designer, you are approached by a salesperson from a floral supplier. You have the following conversation about their products.

> SALESPERSON: As you know, wedding season is fast approaching, and roses are a popular choice for bridal bouquets. We carry a huge selection of roses.
>
> YOU: That's great. Can you tell me about some of the specific varieties and colors you carry?
>
> SALESPERSON: Let's see, we have the pink friendship rose, the yellow Midas touch.... I'll have to get back to you about the other specific varieties we have. As for color, we carry the usual range of white, pink, yellow, and red. We can also do specialty colors.
>
> YOU: How about other flowers and greenery that can be used to fill out a bouquet?
>
> SALESPERSON: Well, we carry baby's breath, which is very inexpensive when purchased in bulk. I should mention that baby's breath is available in a variety of tints. We also have greenery, such as elephant's ear. There's also a new kind of filler plant we just got in, but I can't recall the name at the moment.
>
> YOU: Wonderful. I'd love to know more about the items you carry and your pricing. I will send you an e-mail with some follow-up questions.

Complete the *Pre-Writing Plan* below. Then write the e-mail.

Pre-Writing Plan			
TOPIC	**PURPOSE**	**AUDIENCE**	**FORMAT**
Floral product information			E-mail

SCENARIO B Requesting Delivery Information

You work as a toolmaker at a machine shop. You are waiting for a metal company to deliver the accessories you ordered five days ago. The order includes collet sets, collet chucks, ball bearing drill chucks, and keyed drill chucks. The delivery should have arrived yesterday by close of business, but it did not. You must e-mail the supplier requesting an updated delivery date.

Complete a *Pre-Writing Plan* on your own. Then write the e-mail.

SCENARIO C Requesting Information about Charges

As the manager at a community pool, you are responsible for ordering all the pool-cleaning supplies. Your supervisor leaves you a note about a bill for a shipment of cleaning supplies.

> I noticed that the bill for cleaning supplies this year came to $845. That's about $200 more than last year, and it looks like we ordered the same things. Could you please look into why there has been an increase? Thanks.

You are not sure if prices have increased, if the order has changed from last year, or if there was a billing error. You decide to e-mail the supplier. You want the supplier to explain why the bill has gone up so much.

Complete a *Pre-Writing Plan* on your own. Then write the e-mail.

SCENARIO D Requesting Bids and Quotes

You are a bookkeeper at an auto-supply shop. Recently, the shop decided to purchase vending machines for the office. You must contact several vending machine operators and request quotes for service. You will ask what snack items are available and what they cost. You will also ask how often each company restocks the machines, what it charges for deliveries, and whether it offers any maintenance services. You decide to create a standard business letter that you could send to several different companies.

Complete a *Pre-Writing Plan* on your own. Then create the business letter.

Summary ■ ■ ■

When you write to request information, make sure your reader can easily know exactly what information you need. In particular, keep these points in mind:

- **Clarity** Seemingly minor problems with language and punctuation can have a major impact on the clarity of your message. Reread it carefully before sending.

- **Organization** Use techniques such as bullet points and headings to organize your message.

Answers begin on page 147.

Lesson 16 ▪ ▪ ▪
Offering Feedback

Sometimes employees need to provide positive or critical feedback to another organization. When giving feedback, make sure your message is clear. It is also important to include specific details and to use a polite, respectful tone.

Skill Examples

Suggesting Improvements Michael, an accountant for a software company, calls a supplier. When his call is directed to voice mail, the message identifies the correct extension but the wrong name. Michael decides to tell the supplier about the error. The following examples show how Michael might do this.

Read each example. Then answer the questions that follow.

EXAMPLE 1

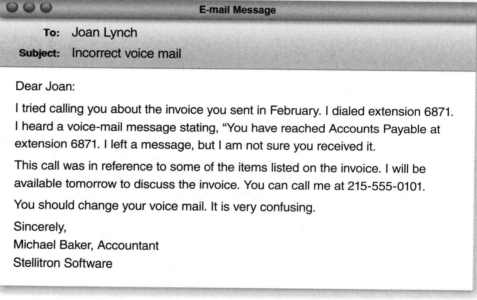

E-mail Message

To: Joan Lynch

Subject: Incorrect voice mail

Dear Joan:

I tried calling you about the invoice you sent in February. I dialed extension 6871. I heard a voice-mail message stating, "You have reached Accounts Payable at extension 6871. I left a message, but I am not sure you received it.

This call was in reference to some of the items listed on the invoice. I will be available tomorrow to discuss the invoice. You can call me at 215-555-0101.

You should change your voice mail. It is very confusing.

Sincerely,
Michael Baker, Accountant
Stellitron Software

1. What question cannot be answered based on Michael's e-mail?

   A. What general issue was Michael calling about?

   B. What extension did Michael call when he tried to reach Joan?

   C. What is the name of the company where Michael works?

   D. What is the phone number where Michael can be contacted?

   E. Which invoice items concern Michael?

2. Which word best describes the tone of the final paragraph?

   F. blunt

   G. happy

   H. worried

   J. sarcastic

   K. apologetic

EXAMPLE 2

```
●●●                    E-mail Message

   To:    Joan Lynch

   Subject:  Incorrect voice mail
```

Dear Joan:

This afternoon, I tried calling you about the invoice you sent to Stellitron Software in February. I dialed your listed extension, 6871, and left a message, but I am not sure that you received it.

The voice-mail message stated, "You have reached Accounts Payable at extension 6871. This is Juan Rodriguez." I just wanted to let you know.

The reason I was calling was to ask about some of the charges listed on the invoice. This is not an urgent matter, but I would like to discuss it this weak if possible. I will be in the office all weak if you would like to give me a call. You can call me at 215-555-0101. Thank you.

Sincerely,
Michael Baker, Accountant
Stellitron Software

Remember!

Spelling When you write a professional e-mail, even small errors can make a poor impression. Using spell-check software will not catch all mistakes, especially those involving homophones. Homophones are words that sound alike but have different spellings and meanings, such as *week* and *weak*. In the third paragraph of *Example 2*, Michael uses the word *weak* incorrectly in two places. He should have used the word *week*.

3. What information would not be clear to the reader of this e-mail?
   A. why Michael is sending an e-mail to Joan
   B. whether Michael needs to talk to Joan right away
   C. when Michael will next be available to talk with Joan
   D. why the voice-mail message was confusing to Michael
   E. what questions Michael has about charges on the invoice

4. What is the likely effect of the statement, "I just wanted to let you know"?
   F. It tells the reader that Michael is very irritated.
   G. It tells the reader that Michael is bossy.
   H. It tells the reader that Michael dialed the wrong number.
   J. It tells the reader that Michael would like an explanation.
   K. It tells the reader that Michael does not think it is a big problem.

Think About It Which example do you feel is more effective? In forming your answer, think about the following questions.

- **Clarity** How should the issue be presented to ensure that the problem is clear to the reader?

- **Tone** What tone is appropriate when pointing out a problem of this nature?

Try It Out!

Writing a Complaint Carla is the human resources manager for a pharmaceutical company. Her supervisor, Earl, sends her an e-mail notifying her of a problem with some employees' insurance cards.

E-mail Message

To: Carla

Subject: Problem with insurance cards

Carla,

In the past week, two employees have complained that their Soundlife Insurance cards were denied by their health care facility.

- Kevin Ling—card number 7041234—was denied on Tuesday, March 15.
- Diane Wills—card number 7041235—was denied on Wednesday, March 16.

I need you to look into this. Please contact Derek Dalton at Soundlife Insurance.

Earl

Carla needs to make it clear that coverage should not have been denied and include details to support this point. Carla uses the *Pre-Writing Plan* to help her.

Pre-Writing Plan			
TOPIC	**PURPOSE**	**AUDIENCE**	**FORMAT**
Employees' insurance cards being denied	To explain problem and request a solution	Representative at health insurance provider	E-mail

Carla wants the problem to be addressed promptly. However, she does not want to offend anyone. She must use a balanced tone—respectful but firm.

E-mail Message

To: Derek Dalton

Subject: Insurance cards being denied for new Farlowe Pharmaceutical employees

Dear Mr. Dalton:

It has come to my attention that several new employees at Farlowe Pharmaceutical are experiencing problems with their Soundlife Insurance cards. The following two employees recently had their cards denied by their health care providers.

- Kevin Ling—card number 7041234—was denied on Tuesday, March 15.
- Diane Wills—card number 7041235—was denied on Wednesday, March 16.

These employees are new hires. However, their insurance should have been effective as of March 1. I can find no explanation for the problem.

Please look into this as soon as possible. Let me know if you need information.

Sincerely,

Carla Goldman

Human Resources Manager, Farlowe Pharmaceutical

Remember!

Organization Using a list with bullet points in an e-mail or letter can organize information and help the reader more easily identify important details. By using bullet points to list the employees' names, card numbers, and dates of denial, Carla has ensured that her reader will know the necessary information in the message.

E-mail is an appropriate **format** for this kind of feedback because it delivers the message quickly and accurately.

Carla addresses her **audience** respectfully throughout the e-mail. Even with complaints, it is best to be polite.

Writing a Complaint Jesse, a high school history teacher, discovers a factual error in a magazine he is using in class. He decides to write a letter to the publisher pointing out the error.

Jesse considers the *Pre-Writing Plan* and then writes the letter.

ADDISON HIGH SCHOOL
204 Lincoln Drive   Anytown, OR 97752

April 4, 2011

Willow Way Publishing Co.
800 21ˢᵗ Street, Suite 501
Noville, NY 10001

To Whom It May Concern:

What's happening in the magazine publishing industry these days? Every year, it seems that more and more errors slip through. This problem goes beyond mere typos to include serious problems with confusing writing, punctuation errors, and factual inaccuracies.

Today I was using your *United States History Magazine* with my tenth-grade history class. On page 43, it refers to the well-known abolitionist William Lloyd Garrison. Unfortunately, it states that he died in 1890. Garrison actually died in 1879. Very few people would even notice an error like that nowadays, but your editors should of found it.

If you want to do something about these errors, that would be great. If not, at least you'll continue to give us a few laughs in the faculty room at Addison High.

Sincerely,
Jesse Barker
Social Studies Department

Write a short response to each item below.

1. How could the first paragraph be revised to make the problem clearer?

2. The final paragraph comes across as though Jesse is talking down to the publisher. Rewrite this paragraph with a more appropriate tone.

Reflect The writers of these examples used the *Pre-Writing Plan* to help them determine which details to include, how to make the messages clear, and what kind of tone to use. Does each message clearly state the problem and suggest what the recipient should do about it? Does each message include the details needed to address the problem? Does each message use a suitable tone?

> **Remember!**
> **Word Choice** Many people incorrectly write *should of* instead of *should have* because the contraction *should've* sounds like *should of*. In the last sentence of the second paragraph, Jesse incorrectly writes *should of*. The correct way to write the sentence is as follows: *Very few people would even notice an error like that nowadays, but your editors should have found it.*

On Your Own ▪ ▪ ▪

Read the following scenarios. Then write your own communications based on
each scenario.

SCENARIO A Informing about a Technical Problem

You are a legislative aide in the office of a state congresswoman who recently had
her website redesigned. You are asked to check it for errors and, if necessary, send
comments to the webmaster. While checking the website, you discover a mistake.
The link to the congresswoman's voting record does not work because the URL
is misspelled.

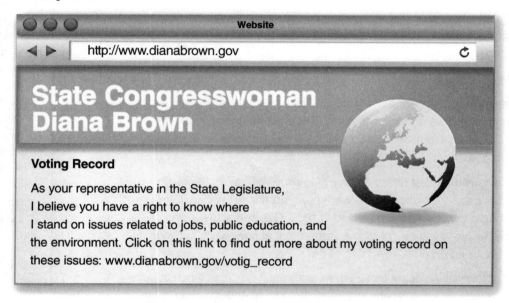

Complete the *Pre-Writing Plan* below. Then write the message.

Pre-Writing Plan			
TOPIC	PURPOSE	AUDIENCE	FORMAT
Broken link on website		Webmaster	

SCENARIO B Expressing a Compliment

As a receiving clerk at a costume shop, you find that the receiving and processing area
of the store is a mess. Boxes are scattered everywhere, and there is little room for new
deliveries. One day, when a delivery arrives, the driver helps you rearrange the space
to make room for the items delivered. You are grateful for this extra help. You decide to
write a letter to the delivery company expressing your appreciation.

Complete a *Pre-Writing Plan* on your own. Decide which details to include and what
tone is appropriate. Then write the letter.

SCENARIO C Writing a Complaint

You work as a night manager for a convenience store. When your cash register stops working one evening, you call a technician. The call does not go well. Later, you decide to write a letter about the poor service. Here is the transcript of the call:

> *MICHELLE: Hi, you've reached Tech Support. This is Michelle.*
> *YOU: Hi, I'm having an emergency problem with our cash register.*
> *MICHELLE: Could you please hold for one moment? [Long pause.] Okay, what is the model number?*
> *YOU: It's CA-942428H. After my last transaction, the drawer locked. I tried punching the "clear" key. I have a line of people waiting.*
> *MICHELLE: I'm going to need to put you on hold again. [Long pause.] Now, what exactly is the problem with your cash register?*
> *YOU: The drawer is locked, I can't reopen it, and I have a line of customers waiting. I tried hitting the "clear" key, but that isn't helping.*
> *MICHELLE: Oh, that's an easy fix. All you need to do is—I'm sorry, could you please hold for a moment? [Long pause.] All right, what you need to do is push the "clear" key and then hold it down for about five seconds.*
> *YOU: Okay, that worked. The drawer is open.*

Complete a *Pre-Writing Plan* on your own. Then write the letter.

SCENARIO D Suggesting Improvement

As a sales associate for a chocolate store at a shopping mall, you have noticed that mall security seems lax. The security guards are employees of an outside security company. They often stand around and talk with one another. You believe they should patrol the mall more. You decide to write a letter to the security company. In it, you should politely ask for clarification of the guards' duties. You could also politely offer suggestions on how you think they could better spend their time.

Complete a *Pre-Writing Plan* on your own. Then write the letter.

Summary ▪ ▪ ▪

When you write to give feedback, make sure your message contains relevant information and is friendly and professional. Keep these points in mind:

- **Clarity** Be sure to state the topic of your communication clearly, whether it is a complaint or praise.

- **Details** Include specific details about the situation you are writing about. This can help the recipient address your particular concerns.

- **Tone** Be polite and respectful, even when you are pointing out a problem. Focus on getting the problem fixed, not on blaming individuals.

Answers begin on page 147.

Lesson 17 ■ ■ ■
Requesting Meetings

Many jobs require employees to arrange meetings with people from other organizations. When you write to request a meeting, you should provide details regarding the purpose for the meeting, the date and time of the meeting, the participants' contact information, and the agenda items. You must also make sure the request is clearly written and logically organized.

Skill Examples

Launching a Project Lucia works as an assistant to the marketing manager of an advertising firm. The manager has asked her to create an agenda for a pre-launch meeting with an important new client. The agenda will be sent to the new client. The following examples show how Lucia might write this.

Read each example. Then answer the questions that follow.

EXAMPLE 1

E-mail Message

To: Meeting Attendees

Subject: Meeting

The pre-launch meeting will take place on March 21 from 9:00 to 3:00 in Conference Room C. Below is the agenda for the meeting. Please review it and contact me with questions.

DISCUSSION ITEMS
- *Overview: Product Identity Package*
- *Marketing Campaigns*
- *Catered Lunch*
- *Wrap-Up*

Lucia

---

1. Which question cannot be answered by reading this agenda?
   A. What is the date of the meeting?
   B. How long will the meeting last?
   C. Will lunch be provided?
   D. What items will be discussed at the meeting?
   E. How should readers contact Lucia with questions?

2. Which of the following details would most improve the agenda?
   F. a menu for the catered lunch
   G. Lucia's last name
   H. more information on the discussion items
   J. the phone number of Lucia's manager
   K. the date of the next meeting

Remember!

Audience When you create an agenda that many people will read, make sure the important information is clear to the entire audience. Lucia's agenda mentions the conference room where the meeting will take place, but that might not be enough information for clients who are unfamiliar with the office. She should include the name of the company, the building, and, if applicable, the floor number.

EXAMPLE 2

Remember!

Capitalization Proper nouns—the names of particular people, places, and things—should always begin with capital letters. In the first sentence of *Example 2*, Lucia should have capitalized the name of the street where the office is located—*Canal Street.* Always proofread your work for correct capitalization.

E-mail Message

To: Pre-Launch Meeting Attendees

Subject: Pre-Launch Meeting Details

The pre-launch meeting will take place on Monday, March 21, from 9:00 A.M. to 3:00 P.M. at our office building at 60 canal street. Please come to Conference Room C, which can be found by taking the East elevator to the third floor. Below is the agenda for our upcoming pre-launch meeting. Please review it carefully and contact me via e-mail or at 949-555-0102 if you have any questions. Thank you.

DISCUSSION ITEMS

9:00–9:30	*Introductions*
9:30–10:30	*Overview:* Product Identity Package for HFC soft drinks
10:30–11:30	*Print Marketing Campaign:* Billboard and Magazine Advertisements
11:30–12:30	*Online Marketing Campaign:* Web and Social Media
12:30–1:45	*Catered Lunch*
1:45–2:45	*Multimedia Campaign:* Television and Radio
2:45–3:00	*Wrap-Up*

Lucia Gomez

---

3. Which question cannot be answered based on this agenda?

A. Who wrote the meeting agenda?

B. What are the names of the employees who will be attending?

C. Where is Conference Room C?

D. How long will the meeting last?

E. What topics will be covered during the print marketing discussion?

4. How are the agenda items organized?

F. by importance

G. by cause and effect

H. with bullet points

J. chronologically

K. in paragraph form

Think About It Which example is more effective for communicating the agenda of the upcoming meeting with the outside organization? In forming your answer, think about the following questions.

- **Details** What specific details should be included in a meeting agenda so that everyone understands what will take place?

- **Organization** How does the way Lucia organized the agenda in *Example 2* make the information clearer than in *Example 1?*

Try It Out!

Proposing a Joint Project Chad Connor, a firefighter, participates in the fire department's community outreach program. The fire chief sends him an e-mail asking him to contact local organizations about meeting to discuss fire safety.

E-mail Message
To: Chad Connor
Subject: Community Outreach Meetings

Chad,

I would like us to expand our Community Outreach program to include other organizations in our community. Please draft a letter that we can send to local schools and businesses to tell them about our program. Let them know we would be happy to meet with them. We will even help them create a fire-escape plan.

Chad realizes that to interest people in the program, he must provide relevant details about it. He uses the *Pre-Writing Plan* to help him.

Pre-Writing Plan			
TOPIC	PURPOSE	AUDIENCE	FORMAT
Fire safety program	To request meetings to discuss fire safety	Leaders of local organizations	Business letter

Chad decides he will start by stating the purpose of his business letter. Then he will use a list to organize details about the program.

Remember!

Sequence Words When you are presenting numerous steps in a condensed form, make sure the sequence is clear. Using sequence words will ensure that the reader understands the message. Sequence words can also display your confidence in the process you describe. Chad uses the words *first, next, during,* and *lastly* to explain exactly how the firehouse's program works.

> The **purpose** is clearly stated in the opening paragraph.

> Chad anticipates questions his **audience** might have.

PLACEVILLE FIRE DEPARTMENT
302 Booker Avenue   Placeville, NC

April 6, 2011

[Organization Name]
[Street address]
[City, State Zip]

Dear [Organization Leader],

I am writing to let you know about the Placeville Fire Department's Community Outreach Program. We would be happy to come and speak to you and your colleagues, free of charge, about fire safety. Here is how our program works:

- First, we send you an outline of our presentation. That way, you can let us know in advance of any additional topics you would like us to cover.
- Next, we schedule two 90-minute presentations on Fire Prevention and Handling Fire Emergencies. During the presentations, we discuss specific safety strategies, such as testing your smoke alarms and using fire extinguishers.
- Lastly, we present you with a fire-emergency plan specific for your building.

Please contact me at 555-0103 if you have any questions. Thank you.

Chad Connor, Firefighter

Proposing a Joint Project Sarah is a labor relations assistant at a sheet metal manufacturer. Her manager asks her to schedule a wage-negotiation meeting between him and a client. He works from 9:00 A.M. to 5:00 P.M. but is unavailable on Tuesday mornings and Friday afternoons.

Sarah considers the *Pre-Writing Plan* and then writes the e-mail.

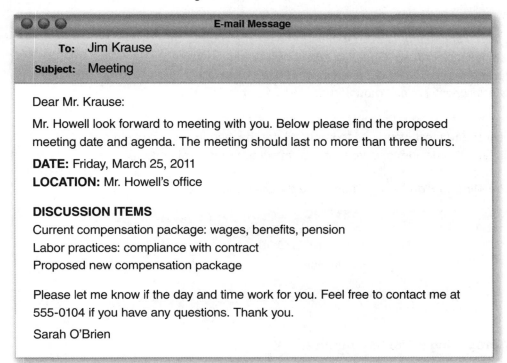

E-mail Message

To: Jim Krause

Subject: Meeting

Dear Mr. Krause:

Mr. Howell look forward to meeting with you. Below please find the proposed meeting date and agenda. The meeting should last no more than three hours.

DATE: Friday, March 25, 2011
LOCATION: Mr. Howell's office

DISCUSSION ITEMS
Current compensation package: wages, benefits, pension
Labor practices: compliance with contract
Proposed new compensation package

Please let me know if the day and time work for you. Feel free to contact me at 555-0104 if you have any questions. Thank you.

Sarah O'Brien

Remember!

Subject-Verb Agreement Make sure that your writing pairs singular verbs with singular subjects and plural verbs with plural subjects. The first sentence of this message uses a plural verb, *look,* with a singular subject, *Mr. Howell.* The sentence should say, "Mr. Howell *looks....*"

Write a short response to each item below.

1. What important detail is missing about when the meeting will take place?

2. The location of the meeting will not be clear if the reader does not know the location of Mr. Howell's office. Rewrite this section to make it clearer.

Reflect The writers of these examples used the *Pre-Writing Plan* to identify their purposes and to help them decide which details to include. Is the purpose of each message clear? Are all the important details provided? Is each message organized clearly?

On Your Own ▪ ■ ▫

Read the following scenarios. Then write your own communications based on each scenario.

SCENARIO A Responding to a Meeting Request

You are a surveyor who is working with an architect in the construction of a neighborhood park. The architect leaves a voice mail requesting a meeting with you.

> *Hi, it's Kathleen. I'm looking forward to meeting with you soon so this project can move forward. We'll need to talk about zoning laws and safety specifications early on. How about if we meet at one o'clock on Wednesday afternoon? Let me know if that works for you. Thanks.*

Before you accept the request, you need to know where the meeting will be held and how long it will last. You decide to write to the architect to request this information.

Complete the *Pre-Writing Plan* below. Then write the message.

Pre-Writing Plan			
TOPIC	PURPOSE	AUDIENCE	FORMAT
	To find out the location and expected duration of the meeting	Architect	

SCENARIO B Proposing a Meeting Request

As a nutritionist, you believe in educating children early about the importance of healthy eating habits. It is a new school year and you decide to contact local school principals to set up some dates when you can come and talk to the students about nutrition. You need to provide details about the kind of information you would share with students and how long your presentation would last. You also want to know if any similar programs are currently in place.

Complete a *Pre-Writing Plan* on your own. Decide which details you need to include and how to organize your inquiry. Then write the message.

SCENARIO C Proposing New Agenda Items

As a wholesale buyer for a furniture store, you often meet with potential suppliers to find high-quality items. Recently, you agreed to meet with a potential furniture supplier. The supplier's representative later sends you the following meeting request.

E-mail Message

To: Farley Furniture
Subject: Meeting

Thank you so much for agreeing to meet with me. Please see the agenda below and let me know if you have any questions. Thank you.

DATE: Monday, March 28
TIME: 3:00 P.M. to 4:30 P.M.
LOCATION: Farley Furniture Store

DISCUSSION ITEMS
Introductions
About Hugh's Wholesale Furniture
Bedroom/Dining Room Sets
Living Room/Home Entertainment

You are available to meet at the proposed place and time. However, you would also like to discuss pricing and delivery. You propose these items in your response.

Complete a *Pre-Writing Plan* on your own. Then write the e-mail.

SCENARIO D Proposing a New Meeting Time

You work as an alarm installer for a small security company. The owner of a new jewelry store informally suggested meeting with you for a consultation. You agreed to do so. However, when the store owner e-mails you a formal meeting request, you realize you are not available at the proposed time. You must write back to her proposing a new time for the meeting.

Complete a *Pre-Writing Plan* on your own. Then write the e-mail.

Summary ▪ ▪ ▪

When you write or respond to a meeting request, consider which information to include and the best way to present it. To do this, keep these points in mind:

▪ **Details** Important details, such as location, time, and proposed items of discussion, must be included when writing to request a meeting.

▪ **Organization** Use headings to help readers find important information, such as the date of a meeting. Discussion items should be organized in a list.

Answers begin on page 148.

Lesson 18 ■ ■ ■
Responding to Queries

In some jobs, you might be required to respond to queries from outside organizations. When you respond to queries, it is important to provide clear answers, include sufficient details, and organize the details logically.

Skill Examples

Responding to a Request for Information As a sales representative for a magazine publisher, Manny receives a query from a bookstore about pricing and delivery schedules. The following examples show how Manny might respond.

Read each example. Then answer the questions that follow.

EXAMPLE 1

● ● ●	E-mail Message
To:	Nothing But Books Bookstore
Subject:	Re: Inquiry about magazines

Thank you for your interest in working with us. In response to your questions:

Pricing
- See the attached chart for national, regional, and niche-market publications.

Delivery
- We deliver weekly magazines on the Saturday of the previous week.
- Monthly magazines are delivered on the 25th of the previous month.
- These schedules allow ample time for you to update displays.
- Quarterly magazines vary. Check with us about specific schedules.
- If an issue sells out a second delivery will be made.

Please feel free to contact me at 1-800-555-0105 if you have any questions.
Manny Jenkins, Sales Representative

1. Which question cannot be answered based on this e-mail and attachment?
   A. On which day of the week are weekly magazines delivered?
   B. How quickly can the distributor provide copies of sold-out magazines?
   C. What are some different types of publications this distributor carries?
   D. What are the prices for the different magazines?
   E. How can the reader find out about quarterly magazines?

2. What information is most likely to persuade a reader to work with Manny?
   F. Weekly magazines are delivered every Saturday.
   G. Monthly magazines are delivered on the 25th of each month.
   H. Delivery schedules vary for quarterly magazines.
   J. Bookstore owners will have time to update displays.
   K. Different types of magazines have different prices.

Remember!

Punctuation Before sending an e-mail, check that the punctuation is correct. In the last bulleted item in *Example 1,* a comma is missing after the word *out,* which makes the sentence hard to read. The sentence should be punctuated like this: *If an issue sells out, a second delivery will be made.* The sentence could also be written this way: *A second delivery will be made if an issue sells out.* Notice that here the comma is not needed.

EXAMPLE 2

E-mail Message

To: Nothing But Books Bookstore
Subject: Re: Inquiry about magazines

Thank you for your recent inquiry concerning Rebbins Distribution's pricing and delivery schedules. As far as pricing is concerned, please see the attached chart for specific publications. In general, the more issues you order for distribution, the better it works out for you. You should probably try to carry many issues of nationally known magazines and just a few copies of lesser-known publications. As for delivery, weekly magazines will come in every Saturday. That should give you enough time. Monthly magazines are delivered on the 25th of each month. For other magazines, the schedule varies alot, so just check with us. You can also let us know any time you sell out of a particular issue.

I hope this information is helpful to you. Please feel free to call me if you have any further questions.

Sincerely,

Manny Jenkins, Sales Representative

Remember!

Spelling Remember to check your spelling before sending a response to an inquiry. The eighth line of *Example 2* contains a common spelling mistake. Manny misspells the phrase *a lot* by incorrectly writing the two words as one word. Errors such as this can make you appear unprofessional.

3. Which question can the reader answer using the information in Manny's e-mail?

   A. What is Manny's phone number?

   B. For what types of magazines does the distribution schedule vary?

   C. Where can the reader find information about pricing for specific magazines?

   D. What will the company do if a bookstore sells out of a magazine?

   E. Why is it better for bookstores to order more issues for distribution?

4. What is the effect of putting all this information in one paragraph?

   F. It helps keep the message focused on one topic.

   G. It shows consideration for the needs of the audience.

   H. It makes the message appear overly formal and cold.

   J. It keeps the topics neatly separated.

   K. It makes it harder for readers to find the information they need.

Think About It Which example more effectively responds to the query? In forming your answer, think about the following questions:

- **Details** What details should be included to ensure that the response fully answers the query?

- **Organization** What techniques can be used to organize information clearly?

Try It Out!

Responding to Queries about Price Changes Fabiana, who owns and runs a small catering company, has recently increased some of her prices. A client sends the following query about an invoice.

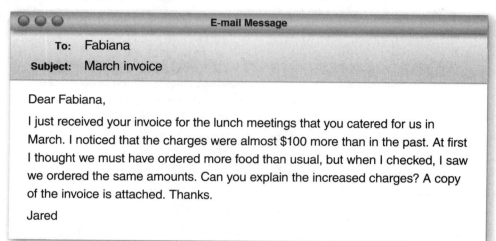

In her response, Fabiana wants to make clear that she raised her prices because the costs of most supplies, such as meat and produce, have risen. She must include specific details to explain this. She uses the *Pre-Writing Plan* to help her.

Pre-Writing Plan			
TOPIC	PURPOSE	AUDIENCE	FORMAT
Query about prices on invoice	To explain why prices have increased	Client company	E-mail

Fabiana decides to organize her response into paragraphs. She knows she should also use a warm, sympathetic tone. Doing so will help her retain this client.

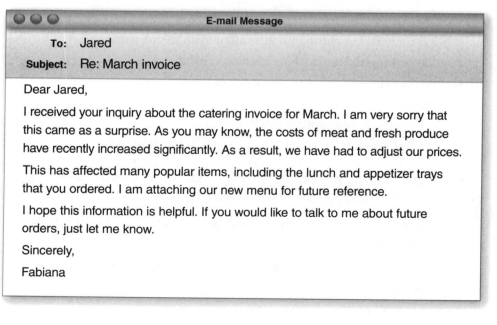

The response is tailored to the **audience's** specific questions and concerns.

The message's tone and details help fulfill the intended **purpose**, which is to explain the price increases while retaining the customer.

Remember!

Transition Words

Transition words can make writing easier to follow by showing how different ideas are connected. For instance, at the end of the first paragraph, the transition phrase *As a result* helps Fabiana explain why she had to raise her prices.

Responding to Queries about Price Changes John, a self-employed jeweler, sells handmade jewelry to a local store. He recently started using higher-quality, more expensive materials, and as a result, has increased his prices. He needs to respond to the store owner's questions about the increase.

John considers the *Pre-Writing Plan* and then sends an e-mail responding to the query.

E-mail Message

To: Annelle's Accessories

Subject: Re: Questions about price increase

Dear Annelle,

Thank you for inquiring about my recent price increases. I apologize if my original message was not clear. In response to your questions:

- No, items using that type of glass bead are not affected by the price increase.
- Yes, items using colored crystals and quartz pendants are affected. The price increase for both items is 10%.

Please understand that I am now working with higher quality, more costly materials. I have had to raise my prices to stay in business. I hope we can continue to work together.

Sincerely,

John Cortland, Owner/Operator—Johnjewels
216-555-0185

Write a short response to each item below.

1. How could the first bullet point be written more clearly?

2. John explains the reason for the price increase, but transition words would make his explanation clearer. Rewrite the first two sentences of the final paragraph. Combine them into one sentence, using the transition word *so* to connect them.

Reflect In the examples on these pages, the writers used the *Pre-Writing Plan* to determine which details to include, how to organize their communications, and how to ensure that each message was clear. Do you think these messages clearly convey information? Is there enough detail? Are the messages organized in a way that makes the relevant information easy to find?

Remember!

Letter Parts Written queries can often result in an extended exchange of communication. It is sometimes easier to discuss things over the phone, so you should include your phone number with all correspondence. In an e-mail, this information can be provided under your name, as in the example on this page. Notice, too, that a formal closing, such as *Sincerely,* is appropriate in a business e-mail.

On Your Own ■ ■ ■

Read the following scenarios. Then write your own communications based on each scenario.

SCENARIO A Responding to Payment Queries

As a payroll clerk at a digital publishing company, you help process payments for freelance writers. A freelancer has e-mailed you to inquire about a late payment. She asked why she has not received payment for work that she invoiced a month ago. You must write to explain that her W-9 tax form is still being processed. She should receive her payment in about two weeks.

Complete the *Pre-Writing Plan* below. Then write the e-mail.

Pre-Writing Plan			
TOPIC	**PURPOSE**	**AUDIENCE**	**FORMAT**
	To explain cause of delay and when payment will be sent		E-mail

SCENARIO B Responding to a Clarification Question

You work as a retail buyer for an electronics store. Recently you sent the following order to a supplier.

ORDER FORM

Electronomarket, Inc.
Name

Street Address   City   State   Zip Code

Item Description	Quantity	Price
E-reader device	5	$1,250.00
Laptop computers	6	$3,000.00
Laser printers		$1,500.00
	Total	$5,750.00

An order clerk at the supplier e-mails you to say your order was not clear. He does not know where to ship the items or how many laser printers you would like to order. You decide to e-mail the clerk with a written explanation of the order.

Complete a *Pre-Writing Plan* on your own. Then write the e-mail.

SCENARIO C Responding to a Request for Information

You manage public relations for a small video-game developer. Your company will soon be releasing a new video game, *Planet Triumph*. Several media organizations have e-mailed you with questions regarding the release. You must create a standard response. It will explain when the game will be released, where it can be purchased, and how many copies will be available.

Complete a *Pre-Writing Plan* on your own. Then write the response.

SCENARIO D Responding to Queries about Delays

You have a job as a dispatcher for a trucking company. A client leaves you the following voice mail about a late shipment.

> *Hi, this is Jim at Office Supplier. We were supposed to receive a shipment of paper products before close of business today. It's now 7:00 P.M., and the shipment hasn't arrived. Can you please let me know when to expect it? I'll be away from my phone so you can e-mail your reply. Thanks.*

Complete a *Pre-Writing Plan* on your own. Decide which details to include and how to organize them. Then write the response.

Summary ■ ■ ■

When you write to answer a query, consider what details your audience needs, how best to organize them, and how to make your response clear. Additionally, keep these points in mind:

- **Clarity** Do not assume that your audience will remember everything they asked about. You may need to restate their questions. At the very least, include all the details of their questions in your answers.

- **Details** Include specific details in response to the questions you were asked. It is better to provide a little too much information than not enough, as long as it is well organized.

- **Organization** Organize information so that it is easy for your audience to find the relevant details. Use bullet points, sequence words, and transitions when appropriate.

Answers begin on page 149.

Job Seeker's Toolkit

The *Job Seeker's Toolkit* is a valuable resource that will help guide you through the job search process. It is full of useful tips and examples. The *Toolkit* will help you identify career options and discover ways to search and apply for jobs. It also provides tips for interviewing and following up after an interview.

Step 1: Explore Careers

Recognize Strengths and Opportunities One of the first actions you need to take in planning a career is to identify your skills. Knowing your strengths and weaknesses will help you match your skills to a suitable job. This includes determining your abilities, skills, preferences, and interests. You also need to identify opportunities by finding fast-growing fields or in-demand careers. Online job sites and newspaper classified ads can help you discover who is hiring and which professions are in demand.

See pages 122–123.

Create a Personal Fact Sheet Making a comprehensive list of your past is one of the most practical things you can do in your job hunt. Putting everything in one document will help you pick the most appropriate items to include in your résumé. In addition, having this document with you when applying for jobs will ensure that you complete your applications quickly and accurately.

Seek Out Additional Education and Training When considering a new job or career, you will need to find out if additional training, experience, or education is required. Taking educational courses or practical training can greatly increase your attractiveness to employers. You must also keep abreast of developments in your areas of interest. Being up-to-date in your field demonstrates your interest in the subject and an eagerness to learn.

Step 2: Search for Jobs

Network Recognize the power of networking in finding and getting a job. Although searching online may help you find a job, many job openings are not publicly advertised. Your best shot at finding these jobs is to build your network of friends and acquaintances—both online and offline. People in your network can serve as references and provide letters of recommendation.

See pages 124–125.

Create an Online Profile An online profile displays your skills and work experience for colleagues and potential employers to see. It is also a way to connect professionally with others and build your network.

Find Job Opportunities Searching online is probably the fastest, easiest, and cheapest way to look for a job. Other good resources include newspaper classified ads, career fairs, temp agencies, and job-search firms. Learning how to tailor your search to find the jobs you want will save you time and make your job search more focused.

Step 3: Apply for Jobs

Create a Résumé Your résumé is often the first exposure a prospective employer has to you. It is therefore vital that both the style and the content of your résumé make you look as impressive as possible. A résumé gives your prospective employer a record of your qualifications, experience, and skills. It can also tell an employer other things about you, such as your attention to detail, your command of language, and your level of creativity.

See pages 126–130.

Write a Cover Letter Along with your résumé, your cover letter creates a first impression of you. Again, style is as important as content here. You need to present information that will convince prospective employers to interview you. You also must write clearly, accurately, and persuasively.

See pages 131–132.

Fill Out a Job Application You may have to fill out an application for a position even if you have submitted a cover letter and a résumé. The application may be on paper or online. This document serves as a record of your personal and professional history. Take the time and effort to make sure it is error-free, accurate, and complete.

See page 133.

Step 4: Interview for Jobs

Use Interview Etiquette Once you have a job interview, you must use that opportunity to promote yourself and get the job. There are several things job seekers should be aware of before they attend an interview.

Answer and Ask Questions Effectively A job interview is not only about answering the interviewer's questions. It is also your opportunity to ask questions about the job and the company. Being prepared for these questions and answers can be the difference between a good interview and a bad one.

Step 5: Follow Up

Write a Thank You Letter After a job interview, be sure to write a thank you letter to the interviewer in a professionally appropriate manner. Even if you are no longer interested in the position, it is important to thank the interviewer for his or her time.

See page 134.

Evaluate and Accept an Offer When you receive a job offer, you must carefully assess it and decide whether to accept it or not. You may want to negotiate the salary and benefits first. Regardless of your decision, you must convey your choice clearly, politely, and professionally.

Write a Follow-up Letter The most professional way to respond to a job offer or rejection is to write a follow-up letter. You should also write a letter if you decide to withdraw your application from consideration at any point during the process.

See pages 135–136.

For more information and practice with the skills related to creating a personal fact sheet, see:

Lesson 1:
Completing Forms

Lesson 3:
Summarizing
Information

Lesson 9:
Preparing Reports

Explore Careers...

Create a Personal Fact Sheet...

When creating a résumé or filling out an application, it is useful to have a record of your personal and professional history. A personal fact sheet is for your reference only, not for an employer. It will help ensure that your résumé and application information is complete and accurate. Having all this information in one place will save you time when applying for jobs.

For security reasons, it is best not to include things like your social security number or driver's license number. You should also omit things that you will not forget, like your name and birth date.

Below is a fact sheet that you can copy and fill out. You may also want to create your own fact sheet.

Always include your current personal information. Update this section when your addresses or phone numbers change.

PERSONAL FACT SHEET

I. Personal Information

Address	
Home Phone Number	
Cell Phone Number	
E-mail Address	

II. Educational Background

Level	Name of School	Type of Degree	Highest Grade/ Level	Dates of Attendance		Scholarships or Honors Received
				From	To	
Elementary						
Junior High or Middle School						
High School						
College						
Other						

III. Work Experience (including non-paid work)

Dates		Position(s) Held	Organization Name, Address, and Phone Number	Monthly Pay	Supervisor's Name
From	To				

IV. Training Programs

Title of Conference/Workshop/ Short Course	Dates of Attendance		Number of Hours	Certificate
	From	To		

V. Other Information

Special Skills/Hobbies	Club/Organization Membership	Other

VI. References

Name	Address	Phone

Include information regarding military service. Be sure to note your dates of service and briefly describe your duties.

If you have received certificates for any training programs, keep copies of these certificates with your personal fact sheet.

Include all of your volunteer work, clubs, memberships, and special skills here. However, when filling out an application, only note the information that relates to the position for which you are applying.

Periodically verify that the contact information for your references is up to date.

For more information and practice with the skills related to creating an online profile, see:

Lesson 1:
Completing Forms

Lesson 3:
Summarizing Information

Lesson 6:
Making Requests

Lesson 10:
Proposing Ideas

Lesson 13:
Expressing Gratitude

Search for Jobs ...

Create an Online Profile ▪▪▪

Creating a profile on a professional networking website is a good way to increase your chances of finding a job, since many companies use these sites to search for job candidates. Having a profile also allows you to connect with friends and colleagues for job leads and support.

An online profile will commonly display your current and past job titles and responsibilities. You also have the option of displaying your contact information. Some networking sites allow you to post your résumé as a document, while others provide a template. Many sites let you include a summary of your skills. You may even be able to post recommendations that others have written for you.

Do some research before selecting a networking site. Some sites cover all jobs and industries. Other sites narrow their focus to specific jobs and industries. Consider creating profiles on a variety of sites. Choose reputable sites that keep your information secure.

Profile ▪▪▪

KEVIN THOMPSON
Administrative Assistant
Anytown, Florida

PROFILE

Kevin Thompson has strong organizational skills, pays close attention to detail, and works well with diverse groups of people. His experiences include maintaining an office, interacting with clients, supervising office interns, and coordinating with outside vendors.

Include a brief summary that describes your skills and job duties across all positions.

Professional Experience:	Administrative Assistant, Sunshine Health Services, Anytown, FL, 2007–present
	Receptionist, Interior Designs Anytown, FL, 2003–2007
	Intern, Interior Designs Anytown, FL, 2002–2003

Connections ⑤

- Clara LaVelle
- Marissa Lopez
- Charles Owen
- Sitara Patel
- Carl Bridges

Interested in:
- Job opportunities
- Finding connections
- Recommendation requests

Most websites allow you to list your purposes.

Connect to both current and former colleagues.

After creating your profile, search the site for colleagues you know and invite them to connect with you. If they accept your invitation, their profile will be linked to your site. Other members may invite you to connect with them. You will receive invitations in your e-mail in-box. Once you accept an invitation, your profile will be linked to their site.

Most professional networking sites have a recommendation feature. Through the website, you can ask people you know to write recommendations for you. These recommendations then become part of your profile, and potential employers can read them.

Invitation ▪ ▪ ▪

E-mail Message

To: Thompson@Sunshinehealth.net

Subject: Connect with me on my network!

Kevin,

Donna Walsh has found you on ConnectWithMe.net.
She would like to add you to her network.

Click here to view and accept the invitation.

Before you accept an invitation, view the member's invitation and profile.

> Invitations are sent via the networking company to safeguard members' privacy.

Recommendations ▪ ▪ ▪

From Donna Walsh, Clinic Manager, Sunshine Health Services

June 12, 2011

"Kevin is one of the most dedicated and competent administrative assistants I have ever supervised. He is not only well organized and efficient but also careful and thorough. His records are always up to date, accurate, and easy to find. Kevin has excellent interpersonal skills. He has been very effective in coordinating with an outside vendor to move all patient records online. Kevin's warmth and humor make him a pleasure to work with."

From Carl Bridges, Owner, Interior Designs, Inc.

December 8, 2010

"Kevin started in our office as an intern and was soon hired as a receptionist. His humor delighted our clients and brightened the workplace. In addition to answering the phone and greeting clients, he began recording payments and organizing files. His great attention to detail became apparent to everyone. Because of his strong interpersonal skills, we also asked him to help train and supervise the interns."

> Online recommendations are similar to standard letters of recommendation but are often shorter.

> Recommendations include the name, title, and company affiliation of the writer, who is also a member of the networking site.

For more information and practice with the skills related to creating a résumé, see:

Lesson 1: Completing Forms

Lesson 3: Summarizing Information

Lesson 9: Preparing Reports

Apply for Jobs . . .

Create a Résumé ■ ■ ■

A résumé is a formal summary of your qualifications and experience. Employers use résumés to screen job applicants. Résumés are typically formatted in chronological, functional, or modified chronological styles. The position you are applying for and your background will help you determine the best style to choose. You will find a sample of each style in the next few pages.

A well-prepared résumé can increase your chances of being called for an interview. Follow these suggestions to create a résumé that will impress prospective employers:

- **Relevance** Tailor your résumé to the position you are applying for and to the company. Be sure to highlight your specific accomplishments. This will show the prospective employer that you are interested in the specific position. This can also help your résumé stand out from more generic ones.

- **Length** Aim for one page in length. Include only the most important information so that the page is not too crowded. Prospective employers will be especially interested in work experience, education, and qualifications that are relevant to the position.

- **Organization** Use informative headings—such as Education and Experience—to define each section of your résumé. This will make your résumé easier to read and will demonstrate your organizational skills.

- **Accuracy** Make sure that everything in your résumé is accurate. Employers often use the contact information in résumés to verify details about your experience. Inaccuracies will create a negative impression and may result in your not being hired. Carefully proofread your résumé for mistakes.

- **Appearance** Make your résumé look professional. Print it on standard-size, good-quality, white paper. Use a standard font and font size.

- **Language** Choose your words carefully to make the greatest impact. Use action words, such as those in the box, to explain your present and past duties. For additional examples of action words, see page 130.

SAMPLE ACTION WORDS

▪ collected	▪ installed	▪ selected
▪ established	▪ provided	▪ sold
▪ helped	▪ recorded	▪ succeeded
▪ interacted	▪ renovated	▪ worked

Chronological Résumé ▪ ■ ▪

A chronological résumé describes your work history in reverse chronological order, listing recent experiences first. This makes it easy for prospective employers to see how your skills and career have developed over time. A chronological résumé is easy to follow and write. However, it can also draw attention to any significant gaps in your employment.

David C. Mikowitz
211 West Jefferson Street
Town, Pennsylvania 55555
(322) 555-1043
dcmiko@email.com

List your name and contact information at the top of the résumé.

OBJECTIVE

To obtain a technical support position, with a special interest in customer service, that will take advantage of my computer and network knowledge and my strong interpersonal skills

Briefly describe the kind of position you are seeking, and highlight your most impressive skills.

EXPERIENCE

Telephone Support Specialist   2007–present
Firefly Cable Company   Town, Pennsylvania

Describe your most recent work experience first.

- Provide thorough and courteous customer support over the telephone for multiple-user platforms and operating systems
- Assist management in developing a training system for new hires
- Consistently beat internal goals for customer satisfaction and amount of time per call

Assistant Information Technology Specialist   2006–2007
Galaxy Publishing   Town, Pennsylvania

Use action words to describe your responsibilities and accomplishments.

- Evaluated and solved individual employee computer issues
- Wrote company handbook for technological support
- Assisted senior staff in troubleshooting internal network issues

EDUCATION

Town Community College   Town, Pennsylvania
2003–2005   *Associate's Degree: Computer Science*

Central High School   Town, Pennsylvania
Graduated 2003

CERTIFICATIONS

Certified Computer Systems Administrator, 2008

Include any certifications that may be relevant to the position.

REFERENCES

Available upon request

Functional Résumé ▪ ▪ ▪

A functional résumé uses headings to highlight your skills and qualifications. Functional résumés are good to use if you want to de-emphasize gaps in your work history or if you have worked briefly for multiple employers. They are also good to use if you are changing careers and want to focus on your skills that can transfer from one job to another, such as the ability to organize, to work with people, or to use computers.

Lorenzo A. Rivera
823 17th Street
Town, Arkansas 55555
(501) 555-1092
lorenzor@email.com

EMPLOYMENT OBJECTIVE
Experienced and dependable worker with own truck and tools looking for maintenance or construction work

SKILLS AND QUALIFICATIONS

Framing and Roofing
- Ten years of experience in all aspects of commercial and residential construction
- Construct wood and metal frames
- Build and repair shingle, rubber, and steel roofs

Electrical Work and Plumbing
- Install and repair electrical systems in commercial and residential buildings
- Install toilets, sinks, and showers
- Reroute existing piping

Painting
- Fifteen years of experience painting interiors and exteriors
- Excel at brush, roll, and spray painting, as well as detailed finish work

EDUCATION
Plumbing Certification
High School Diploma   Central High School, Town, Arkansas

EMPLOYMENT HISTORY
Standard Construction Company   1999–2009
City, Arkansas

Able Painting   1980–1995
City, Arkansas

REFERENCES
Available upon request

Use headings to identify groups of skills.

Use action verbs to emphasize your skills and experiences.

Do not include a graduation date if you are concerned about age discrimination.

Modified Chronological Résumé ■ ■ ■

A modified chronological résumé combines the chronological and functional résumé styles. It is a good choice if you want to group similar skills together and you do not need to de-emphasize gaps in your employment history. Grouping similar skills together allows you to move important experiences to the top of your résumé even if the experiences are not recent.

Andrea Kim

1822 Read Street, Town, Oregon 55555   akim@email.com   (971) 555-1033

OBJECTIVE
Computer-savvy office worker with a positive attitude seeks a clerical position to utilize strong organizational and interpersonal skills.

COMPUTER SKILLS

Administrative Assistant, **Clearwater Agencies**   January 2008–present
Town, Oregon
- Perform tasks using word-processing, spreadsheet, and presentation software, several internet browsers, and multiple graphic software programs
- Research, implement, and maintain revised structure for company database
- Train new employees on use of computer systems and software

Office Assistant, **Systems Inc.**   April 2006–December 2008
Town, Oregon
- Worked with a variety of operating systems, internal and external drives, and various printer configurations

ORGANIZATIONAL SKILLS

Administrative Assistant, **Clearwater Agencies**   January 2008–present
Town, Oregon
- Reformatted company database for ease of navigation
- Created file-naming and file-archiving system
- Coordinate company events, including sending invitations, catering, and booking entertainment

INTERPERSONAL SKILLS

Administrative Assistant, **Clearwater Agencies**   January 2008–present
Town, Oregon
- Interact effectively with coworkers, clients, other organizations, and vendors
- Recognized as Employee of the Month several times for outstanding interpersonal and organizational skills

Volunteer, **Friends of the Library**   May 2005–present
Town, Oregon
- Assist head librarian with community outreach program
- Gathered signatures for successful proposal to increase library hours

EDUCATION
Diploma, **Central High School**   2006
Town, Oregon

REFERENCES
Available upon request

Briefly describe your skills, experience, relevant personality traits, and the kind of position you are seeking.

List specific skills and qualifications under more general skill headings.

List specific accomplishments.

Key Action Words ▪ ▪ ▪

Use strong, specific verbs such as those listed below to describe your skills and responsibilities. You can also consult a dictionary or thesaurus for ideas.

advised	earned	planned
analyzed	edited	presented
approved	evaluated	produced
arranged	examined	recommended
assembled	executed	referred
assessed	facilitated	remodeled
assisted	filed	repaired
attained	gathered	represented
attended	generated	researched
audited	guided	responded
budgeted	handled	saved
built	identified	scheduled
calculated	implemented	screened
carried out	improved	served
clarified	initiated	shaped
classified	inspected	solved
communicated	instructed	started
compiled	interpreted	structured
completed	introduced	studied
conducted	maintained	summarized
contacted	managed	supervised
coordinated	marketed	supported
created	obtained	trained
delivered	operated	translated
demonstrated	ordered	typed
designed	organized	upgraded
developed	oversaw	volunteered
directed	participated	won
distributed	performed	wrote

Write a Cover Letter ▪ ▪ ▪

A cover letter is a business letter addressed to a potential employer. It accompanies a résumé and provides important information about the writer. Think of a cover letter as a way to introduce yourself to a potential employer. It can also be used to highlight, explain, or expand on parts of your résumé. Your cover letter is your chance to let your personality shine. You can explain, in your own words, why you are the right person for the job.

Keep the length of your cover letter to one page, and proofread it carefully for grammar and spelling errors. You want your reader to see you as a competent, responsible professional.

For more information and practice with the skills related to writing a cover letter, see:

Lesson 5: Expressing Opinions

Calvin James
823 17th Street
Town, Pennsylvania 55555

> Include your name and address at the top of the cover letter.

March 29, 2011

Mr. Luis Perez
West End Apartments
8928 West Warren Street
Town, Pennsylvania 55555

> Address your cover letter to a specific person rather than a general title, such as "Hiring Manager." Also include the name and address of the company.

Dear Mr. Perez:

Your tenant Andre Johnson recommended that I contact you about the maintenance supervisor position you are seeking to fill. I believe I am well qualified to deliver the services that you and your tenants need.

> The first paragraph should state your reason for writing, the position you are applying for, and how you heard of the job opening. This information will not be in your résumé and may be of interest to your reader.

I have several years of experience in various construction fields and a plumbing certification. In addition, I have the tools and knowledge to handle just about any structural issue that your apartment buildings might have. I can install and repair air conditioners, furnaces, water heaters, ceiling fans, and appliances. I can remove and install carpeting and flooring. I can also repair apartment damage and prep apartments to look like new.

> Explain why you are the right person for the job. This is a good opportunity to elaborate on the information in your résumé.

If you contact my references, you will find that I have a reputation for being honest, hard-working, and reliable. I am also easy to work with and friendly.

I have enclosed my résumé and a list of references. I would greatly appreciate meeting with you to discuss this position further. I can be reached by phone (406-555-0103) or by e-mail (calvinj@email.com).

> Mention that your résumé is enclosed, and be sure to ask for an interview. Give the employer at least one way to reach you.

Thank you for your time.

Sincerely,

Calvin James

> Use black or blue ink for your signature. Type your name below your signature.

Calvin James

When applying for a job for which you have little or no professional experience, focus on your education or the skills that would make you a good candidate for the job.

Alice Abbad
1929 Caldon Street
Town, Iowa 55555
(967) 555-0198
aliceab@email.com

June 17, 2011

Include the date that the letter is being sent.

Ms. Janelle Stevens
92.1 FM
92 Queen Street
Town, Iowa 55555

Dear Ms. Stevens: Use a formal greeting.

Cover letters do not always have to be sent in response to job postings. It is often a good idea to contact potential employers and let them know you would like to work for them.

I would like to express my interest in an entry-level position with 92.1 FM. I am a recent graduate with a degree in broadcast journalism, and I am interested in working for a station that I greatly respect.

I have a clear, confident voice and a passion for current events. I have a history of learning quickly and working well within a team. I would be glad to share my portfolio with you, which showcases some broadcasting projects I completed in college.

When you have no relevant professional experience, highlight your education, special skills, personal traits, and any non-paid experience you might have.

During my senior year in college, I was selected for a prestigious broadcast internship with 101.9 FM. There I became acquainted with the processes and protocols of working in a radio station.

Please review my enclosed résumé. I would appreciate the opportunity to speak with you in person about the positive contributions I can make to the 92.1 FM team. I can be reached any time by phone (967-555-0198) or e-mail (aliceab@email.com).

Thank you very much for your time.

Sincerely,

Alice Abbad

Alice Abbad

Mention your enclosed résumé. Let employers know that you would like to meet with them. Make it as convenient as possible for them to contact you.

Fill Out a Job Application ▪ ▪ ▪

Many companies will require you to complete a job application. Job applications may be paper or online. They may include topics that are not addressed in your résumé or cover letter. Follow these suggestions to ensure that your job application makes a good impression:

- Be prepared. Bring your personal fact sheet and a pen with black or blue ink.

- Scan the entire application before writing. Follow the directions carefully, and print neatly.

- Be thorough. Do not leave blank spaces in the application. Write *n/a* (for *not applicable*) if a question does not apply to you.

- Be honest. You may not want to answer questions that reveal negative information about you. However, giving false information can cause problems for you in the future. You could even lose your job. One option is to write *willing to discuss* on the line.

- Include as much positive information about yourself as you can. In addition to your work experience and education, include volunteer work, military service, and relevant hobbies.

- Proofread your application for errors in spelling, grammar, capitalization, and punctuation.

For more information and practice with the skills related to filling out a job application, see:

Lesson 1:
Completing Forms

Lesson 4:
Writing Instructions and Guidelines

Last Name	First Name	Middle Initial	
Sutton	Elizabeth	E.	
Street Address		**City, State, Zip**	
122 Wallace Court		Township, NJ 10555	
Phone Number	(102) 555-1024	**Social Security Number**	123-45-6789
Position Desired	Cashier	**Pay Desired**	$8 per hour
Date Available for Work	Now	**Hours Available**	Weekdays after 4
Are you a U.S. citizen?	Yes	**Have you ever been convicted of a felony?**	No
Education (highest)	Dawson High School	**Degree or Diploma**	Diploma
EMPLOYMENT HISTORY (List most recent employer first.)			
Employer	Seaside Books	**Position**	Cashier
Address	123 Main Street, City, NJ 02222	**Dates**	October 2009- November 2011
Phone	215-555-1286	**Supervisor**	Karen Slade

Write a Thank You Letter ▪ ▪ ▪

For more information and practice with the skills related to writing thank you letters, see:

Lesson 3:
Summarizing Information

Lesson 5:
Expressing Opinions

Lesson 6:
Making Requests

Lesson 10:
Proposing Ideas

Lesson 13:
Expressing Gratitude

It is important to write a brief thank you letter within a day or two after a job interview. This helps keep you in your potential employer's mind. It also demonstrates professional courtesy and an ability to communicate well.

In your letter, thank the interviewer for the meeting, and express your continued interest in the position. Maintain a professional, optimistic, and respectful tone. For most jobs, use a business-letter format to create your letter. For informal or creative workplaces, however, e-mail or handwritten letters may be acceptable.

Leanne Silver
102 East Street
City, Illinois 55555
(215) 555-1036
lsilver@email.com

Include the date that the letter is being sent.

April 23, 2011

Include the name and title of the person you interviewed with and the company address.

Mr. Daniel Johnson
Director, Superior Designs
24 Riverview Road
City, Illinois 55555

Dear Mr. Johnson:

The first paragraph should thank the interviewer. Include the date of the interview and the position you applied for.

Thank you for taking the time to meet with me on Tuesday, April 22, about the office manager position. I enjoyed talking with you and hearing about your creative vision for Superior Designs.

Confirm your understanding of the position, and briefly restate your qualifications.

I believe that my skills and experience are well matched for the position. My strong organizational skills will help ensure that the design team is well prepared for its many presentations to clients. My experience with maintaining budgets and schedules can help increase office efficiency.

Convey your strong interest, and let the interviewer know the best way to reach you for further communication.

I am excited about the many facets of the position and greatly interested in working for your company. Please feel free to contact me if you need additional information. My cell phone number is 215-555-1036. I look forward to hearing from you.

Thank you for your time.

Sincerely,

Leanne Silver

Use black or blue ink for your signature. Type your name below your signature.

Leanne Silver

Write a Follow-up Letter ∎ ∎ ∎

A follow-up letter is the most professional way to respond to a job offer or rejection or to withdraw an application from consideration. Send a follow-up letter for each of these purposes:

- **To accept** Confirm your understanding of the offer by restating its terms, and ask any questions. Convey your enthusiasm to your new employer.

- **To decline** Write a letter thanking the company for the offer. Briefly explain a few factors that affected your decision. Do not write anything negative, since you may want to contact the company in the future.

For more information and practice with the skills related to writing follow-up letters, see:

Lesson 3:
Summarizing Information

Lesson 5:
Expressing Opinions

Lesson 6:
Making Requests

Lesson 10:
Proposing Ideas

Lesson 13:
Expressing Gratitude

Jason Jenkins

29 West Front Street   (707) 555-0123
City, California 55555   Jjenkins@email.com

April 30, 2011

Ms. Angela Keller
Director, Classy Catering
33 Ocean Highway
City, California 55555

Dear Ms. Keller: Use a formal greeting.

Thank you for offering me the position of manager with Classy Catering. I am happy to accept this position.

I look forward to starting with the company on Monday, May 1, at 8:00 A.M. I will meet you at the main office, wearing business casual clothing. My understanding is that I will be working 40 hours per week, at a salary of $30,000 per year. After 30 days, I will qualify for the benefits package. This includes one week of paid vacation the first year and two weeks of paid vacation in the following years.

Again, thank you for this excellent opportunity. I look forward to working with you.

Sincerely,

Jason Jenkins

Jason Jenkins

Include your name and contact information at the top of the letter.

In the first paragraph, thank the company for the job offer and clearly accept the position.

Restate the terms of the offer, including start date, salary, hours, benefits, and any other relevant information.

Express your gratitude and enthusiasm. Be sure to maintain a professional tone.

You should also send a follow-up letter for these purposes:

- **To respond to a rejection** Thank the employer for considering you, and express your continued interest in the company. Your response could position you to be considered for that company's next job opening.

- **To withdraw from the process** Write a letter withdrawing yourself from consideration. Explain your decision in a positive way.

Alicia Taylor
15 Dean Street
City, California 55555
(727) 555-1024
ataylor@email.com

April 30, 2011

Mr. Mark Burnett
Burnett Garden Center
55 Hillside Avenue
City, California 55555

> Include the name and title of the person you met with.

Dear Mr. Burnett:

> **Acknowledge that you have not been hired, and thank the company for considering you. If you received a letter or e-mail, refer to it.**

I just learned that you have selected another candidate for the position of sales associate. Although I am disappointed, I want to thank you for considering me and for your courtesy throughout the process.

> **Express your continued interest in the position, and give one or two reasons why you respect the company.**

I am very glad that I had the opportunity to meet with you and learn more about your company. I was very impressed by your commitment to quality and your emphasis on customer service. Please know that I continue to be very interested in working at the garden center.

> **Ask to be considered for future positions, and express positive feelings toward the company.**

Please keep me in mind when you have other job openings. In the meantime, I wish you and the company the very best.

Sincerely,

Alicia Taylor

Alicia Taylor

Answer Key ■ ■ ■

Lesson 1 (pp. 6–11)

Skill Examples
1. A   2. H   3. B   4. G

Think About It
Example 2 is more effective. <u>DETAILS:</u> *Example 2* includes all of the details needed to ensure that the message reaches its intended recipient and that the recipient can easily contact Rhonda. For example, it includes both the sender's and the recipient's names and contact information. *Example 1* is missing the recipient's name. <u>TONE:</u> *Example 1* uses informal language and an inappropriate exclamation point. *Example 2* uses an appropriately professional tone.

Try It Out!
Possible Answers
1. Anthony could remove the detail about how dropping the boxes got everyone's attention. He also does not need to use this form to apologize or offer to pay for the damage. He can discuss those details with his manager.
2. When the box hit the floor, it made a loud noise. This got the attention of customers and staff.

Reflect
Answers should include reasons explaining whether each example is clear and detailed and has an appropriate tone. The first example has a clear message, effectively conveys relevant details, and uses standard English throughout. The second example provides a lot of information, but is less effective because it includes irrelevant details and uses informal language.

On Your Own
See Writing Rubric on page 150

Scenario A
Topic: Tracking workday details

Purpose: To describe the employee's hours worked and tasks completed

The work log should include **details** about which cases the employee worked on. To be **clear**, the explanation should also identify which tasks were completed, and how many hours were allotted to different cases and tasks. The **tone** should be objective and professional.

Scenario B
The explanation should be **clear** and include **details** describing the damage to the suitcase and how the damage occurred. The **tone** should be neutral and professional. Information should be presented objectively and in standard English.

Scenario C
All of the **details** provided in the scenario (the customer's and recipient's names, date, and so on) should be included in the delivery form students have created. To ensure that the customer's preferences are **clear**, the explanation at the bottom should note that the customer ordered yellow roses instead of pink. The request for a morning delivery time should also be noted. The **tone** should be objective and professional, and standard English should be used throughout the form.

Scenario D
To ensure that the sender, subject, and intended recipient are **clear**, the fax cover sheet should include the following fields: sender, recipient, fax numbers for sender and recipient, subject line, and number of pages. These fields should be completed with the relevant **details**. Additionally, details about the items ordered should be included on the cover sheet, or the cover sheet should direct the recipient to see the attached order form. The **tone** of the message should be friendly and professional. Any notes on the cover sheet should use standard English and avoid slang.

Lesson 2 (pp. 12–17)

Skill Examples
1. C   2. J   3. E   4. H

Think About It
Example 2 is more effective. <u>AUDIENCE:</u> Busy employees might scan the e-mail in *Example 1* and conclude from the overuse of capital letters and exclamation points and the omission of a specific date that they must go outside immediately. In *Example 2*, the employees are told when the drill will occur. Capitalization, underlining, and boldfacing also make it easy to see the important points. <u>DETAILS:</u> *Example 2* includes the necessary details for the fire drill: who must take part, when it will be held, why it will be held, and what people should do during it.

Try It Out!
Possible Answers
1. Sergio could have given the phone number of the Help Line.
2. I called the Help Line at noon, and they said they would be here before 3:00 P.M.

Reflect

Answers should include the reasons the formats are effective or ineffective and a discussion of details included or omitted. In *Example 1,* Tim uses an e-mail to get the message out to everyone and posts the notice where the intended audience will see it. In *Example 2,* Sergio posts the notice appropriately, but an e-mail would also have been helpful. Other appropriate formats for reminders are newsletters, websites, and memos. *Example 1* also includes all the details needed, while *Example 2* omits the time the Help Line was called and the phone number.

On Your Own

See Writing Rubric on page 150

Scenario A

Topic: Thefts in area offices

Purpose: To remind staff to secure their belongings

The e-mail should include all the key **details**, such as when, where, and how the thefts occurred. It should also list the specific things that workers should do to avoid theft and what they should do if they are the victim of theft. Security's phone number should be noted. Bullet points would help organize this information. The e-mail should NOT contain unnecessary information, such as Mark's comment about the ridiculousness of not using locks.

Scenario B

Not everyone responded to the first notice, so an e-mail would probably be the best **format** to reach your intended **audience**. It could be accompanied by another notice, which should be clear and prominently displayed at the restaurant. The message should include all the key **details**, such as when and how employees should respond.

Scenario C

An e-mail would probably be the best **format**. The **audience** should be everyone who submits time sheets. The message should include these **details:** when readers should submit time sheets and why they need to do this early. It should stress that time sheets should be submitted to Keira, not to Conrad. The message should NOT include the comment about Conrad being swamped.

Scenario D

The **audience** should be all employees. **Details** should include exactly when the refrigerator will be cleaned and what will be done with items still in the refrigerator. The tone should be friendly and cooperative. An offer could be made to work out a plan with anyone who feels inconvenienced by this cleaning.

Lesson 3 (pp. 18–23)

Skill Examples

1. D   2. K   3. E   4. F

Think About It

Example 2 is more effective. <u>DETAILS:</u> *Example 2* includes all the details Donna wanted employees to know, including whether the office is open tomorrow and the fact that Donna can be reached by e-mail. *Example 1* omits those details and inappropriately includes Donna's comment about the effect of the snowy day on profits. <u>ORGANIZATION:</u> *Example 1* is not organized in a way that helps clarify the information. The use of bullet points in *Example 2* clearly identifies the important points.

Try It Out!

Possible Answers

1. The writer could organize the job duties using headings, such as *Covering Your Workstation, Handling Customer Calls,* and *Maintaining the Computer Log.* Each heading could then contain specific information using bullet points.

2. Arrange for someone to cover your workstation when you take breaks.

Reflect

Answers should focus on the details included in each description, along with the techniques used to organize each. Answers should connect the details and organization to each description's purpose. Both examples include relevant details, but the first example's organization—the use of headings—better fits the purpose.

On Your Own

See Writing Rubric on page 150

Scenario A

Purpose: To provide details about the crime and the police officer's conclusions

Format: Incident report

The incident description should include the following **details:** the names of the police officer and store manager, the place and time of the burglary, a list of stolen merchandise along with its value. The description should also include the officer's conclusion involving the unlocked back door. This information should be **organized** in paragraphs. Bullet points or numbers as well as sequence words may be used.

Scenario B

The message should be brief and should include the following **details:** the name of the day care center and a few sentences describing the malfunctioning air conditioning system. The location and contact details should be identified at the beginning, while the details can be **organized** in paragraphs.

Scenario C
The letter should include the following **details**: the fact that the invoices are included, an explanation of each invoice, and a statement that the apartment complex should disregard the bills if it has sent in its payment. The letter should be **organized** in paragraph form with a greeting.

Scenario D
The summary should include the key **details** the manager presented: specifically, the necessity of storing items in the proper refrigerator, washing knives and cutting surfaces, and using the green cleaning solution. This will help ensure that the new rules are clear to employees. The summary can be **organized** using an introductory paragraph followed by headings, such as *Refrigeration* and *Cleanliness*. Appropriate information can be listed below each heading, using bullet points.

Lesson 4 (pp. 24–29)

Skill Examples
1. A   2. H   3. D   4. J

Think About It
Example 2 is clearer. <u>ORGANIZATION:</u> *Example 2* uses bullet points and sequence words effectively to organize the steps. This helps ensure that the employee will complete the steps in order. Because the order of steps is less clear in *Example 1*, the employee may complete some steps out of order. <u>CLARITY:</u> In *Example 2*, Reggie could have used numbers instead of bullet points for the steps. If he had, sequence words would not have been necessary.

Try It Out!
Possible Answers
1. Janet could have organized the list using bullet points, since the order of the items is not particularly important.
2. Always be cheerful, friendly, and polite when interacting with our clients.

Reflect
Answers should discuss the organization and clarity of each example. In *Example 1* bold headings and bullet points help organize information effectively, and the language is clear and specific. In *Example 2*, vague language, such as *good behavior*, makes the writing less clear. The code is effectively organized.

On Your Own
See Writing Rubric on page 150

Scenario A
Topic: Assisting guests with luggage

Purpose: To provide instructions to bellhops explaining how they should assist guests

To ensure that the instructions are **clear** to the new bellhops, the procedure should list, step by step, the bellhops' duties. Sequence words or a numbered list should be used to **organize** the steps; for example, *The first thing bellhops should do is approach guests and offer to assist them with their luggage. Then . . . .*

Scenario B
The procedure should be **organized** as a list of steps explaining what the assistant should do before, during, and after the party. A numbered list or sequence words would add **clarity** to the process. The steps should be written with simple and direct language, using parallel structure.

Scenario C
Responses should present the steps for arming and disarming the security system in a logical way. To ensure that the instructions are **clear,** list separately the steps for arming and for disarming the system. The response should be **organized** as a list of numbered or bulleted steps.

Scenario D
To make the guidelines **clear,** they should be **organized** according to the following key points: on which day each break room should be restocked, how often items should be restocked, and which items need to be restocked. These are simple guidelines, so bullet points can be used but are not necessary.

Lesson 5 (pp. 32–37)

Skill Examples
1. B   2. G   3. A   4. K

Think About It
Example 1 is more effective. <u>DETAILS:</u> *Example 1* states Hannah's main objection to the proposed change and then supports her objection with details about customers' preferences and the potential impact on customer service. In *Example 2*, the second sentence contains irrelevant information, and the next to the last sentence does not provide any new details and is overstated. <u>TONE:</u> In *Example 1*, Hannah maintains a polite and professional tone. Even though she disagrees with the proposed policy, she thanks her supervisor for giving her the opportunity to provide feedback. In *Example 2*, she uses phrases, such as *bad idea, waste of time, way too busy,* and *crazy idea,* which are disrespectful and unprofessional.

Try It Out!

Possible Answers

1. Following the third sentence, Ahmet could explain why he thinks wearing casual clothing is inappropriate.

2. I do not think this policy is appropriate.

Reflect

Answers should include reasons to explain how each writer did or did not achieve his purpose. The first communication uses a positive and professional tone. The second is too abrupt and uses a question where a statement would be more effective. The first e-mail uses details to answer specific questions. The second e-mail would be more effective if Ahmet stated his reasons for concern and supported them with details.

On Your Own

See Writing Rubric on page 150

Scenario A

Topic: Supervisor's request that employee work overtime

Purpose: To explain that the employee cannot work over the weekend but can work extra hours next week

The e-mail should include the key **details**, briefly explaining why the employee cannot work this weekend, agreeing to work extra hours the following week, and reassuring the supervisor that the work will be completed on time. The **tone** should be polite and professional. Ending on a positive note ("I am confident that I can complete the orders by Friday.") would help reassure the supervisor.

Scenario B

The employee's response should include specific **details** about the volume of work that the shipping department completes, how other employees have helped in the past, and how changing the policy might affect order-processing time. The message should present the employee's objections in a serious, respectful, and professional **tone.**

Scenario C

The note should include specific **details** about the employee's two main concerns about the move: the impact on employee parking and the impact on the animals. The **tone** of the message should be respectful and polite, but the message must nevertheless state the employee's objections openly. Objective, neutral language would help accomplish this.

Scenario D

The e-mail should include **details** about the writer's continued interest in the job and appreciation of the offer. It should also include a statement of the salary the writer expects, supported with details about

typical industry salaries and the writer's prior experience. The writer's **tone** should be polite, reasonable, and cooperative. The writer should not sound disappointed or insulted by the salary offer.

Lesson 6 (pp. 38–43)

Skill Examples

1. B   2. J   3. B   4. K

Think About It

Example 2 is more effective. DETAILS: *Example 2* provides specific details about what date Marion needs off, who can take over her shift, and how this will be accomplished while having full coverage on both shifts. *Example 1* provides incomplete details, making it more difficult for the supervisor to accommodate the request. TONE: In *Example 2,* the phrases *I would like to request* and *Please let me know* are appropriate for making a request. In *Example 1,* the phrase *I will have to* is inappropriate since it does not actually make the request and asserts the need for time off as though that is enough.

Try It Out!

Possible Answers

1. *Hi, you guys, super fun, total stand-up guy, awesome*

2. I think I have shown that I am dependable, hardworking, and dedicated.

Reflect

Answers should include information on how each writer deals with details, organization, and tone. The first example presents specific details, organizes them in a numbered list, and maintains a positive, professional, and respectful tone. The second example could include more specific details about Mason's value as an employee. The tone is respectful and positive but should be more formal.

On Your Own

See Writing Rubric on page 150

Scenario A

Topic: Questions about writing a report on the Armstrong case

Format: E-mail or a brief typed note

The message should include **details** about several points on which the employee needs clarification: which files are needed, who can provide them, what template is used for reports, who will review the document, and when the report is needed. The employee could **organize** the message with a brief introductory statement followed by a list of bullet points or a numbered list of questions. The **tone** should be respectful and professional. The employee should NOT discuss his or her inexperience but rather point out the importance of obtaining the requested information to complete the task successfully.

Scenario B

The employee's response should include **details** showing why extra help is needed. For example, the number of accounts assigned exceeds the employee's typical weekly workload. The employee should also include details about how much assistance is needed. The message could be **organized** in one or two brief paragraphs. The **tone** of the message should be polite and respectful. The employee should sound objective, not frustrated or resentful.

Scenario C

The notice should include specific **details** about which scheduled shifts the employee needs to have covered and which shifts the employee can pick up the following week. These points could be **organized** in a brief paragraph. A list could be used if multiple shifts are mentioned. The **tone** of the message should be polite and respectful.

Scenario D

The e-mail should include **details** about points the employee would like to know more about, such as the qualifications required, the nature of the job duties, and the application process. Since the request is being sent to a manager in another department, it should be **organized** to include a formal greeting, body paragraphs, a closing, and name. The writer's **tone** should be formal and professional.

Lesson 7 (pp. 44–49)

Skill Examples

1. D   2. F   3. E   4. G

Think About It

Example 2 is more effective. <u>TONE:</u> When responding to criticism, employees should use an objective, professional tone, as Troy does in *Example 2*. They should avoid sounding defensive, as Troy does in *Example 1*. <u>ORGANIZATION:</u> *Example 2* uses clearer organization, which shows Troy's thoughtful response to the criticism. *Example 2* also uses organization to highlight Troy's positive traits, as pointed out in question 4.

Try It Out!

Possible Answers

1. Alex could move the details addressing the passengers' specific complaints from the middle of the paragraph to the first sentence.

2. If you would like to discuss this issue further, please let me know.

Reflect

Answers should include a discussion of how the writers organized their communications and how their language choices affect the tone. The first writer gives a detailed description of the problem and a suggestion for addressing it. The second writer states the problem vaguely. He then describes his actions in detail before explaining the problem. The structure of the second example makes it difficult to follow. The language in the first example helps convey a polite, formal, and serious tone. The casual language in the second example makes the writer appear less serious.

On Your Own

See Writing Rubric on page 150

Scenario A

Topic: Customer's complaint

Purpose: To request guidance on how to best resolve the problem

The message should use an objective **tone** in explaining the problem, briefly apologizing, and requesting advice. The employee should take care not to sound defensive. The employee's **purpose** is to summarize the problem and ask the supervisor for advice. The employee can **organize** the message in two brief paragraphs addressing those two points.

Scenario B

The employee's **tone** should be sincerely apologetic and helpful as he or she proposes a solution to the problem. The employee's **purpose** is to acknowledge the problem, apologize for it, and suggest a solution. The message could be **organized** in two brief paragraphs. The first paragraph would sum up the problem and present the employee's apology.

Scenario C

The employee's **tone** should be neutral in requesting clarification. Since the employee heard the criticism secondhand, it is not appropriate to apologize for or explain the clean-up procedure. The **purpose** of the memo is to determine what procedure the supervisor prefers. The memo could be **organized** in two brief paragraphs, summing up the concern raised by the coworker and then requesting clarification.

Scenario D

The employee's **tone** should be polite and apologetic in presenting the problem. The employee's **purpose** is to explain the reason for the sales decision and to demonstrate his or her determination not to repeat the mistake. This purpose could be accomplished by **organizing** the note in two brief paragraphs. The first paragraph should summarize what happened. The second paragraph should include an apology and a promise to handle future situations differently.

Lesson 8 (pp. 50–55)

Skill Examples

1. B   **2.** H   **3.** B   **4.** H

Think About It

Example 2 is more effective. <u>ORGANIZATION:</u> Jimmy's purposes are to present his concerns and to request changes. *Example 2* is organized clearly. The first paragraph states Jimmy's purposes. The second and third paragraphs address his concerns and propose solutions. The final paragraph requests a specific next action and thanks the supervisor for considering the issue. *Example 1* is less organized. It does not state Jimmy's purposes. It also presents his first request before explaining his concern. <u>DETAILS:</u> In *Example 1*, Jimmy includes some relevant details but does not mention where signs could be posted or that workers have had to buy their own safety equipment. Jimmy includes this information in *Example 2*.

Try It Out!

Possible Answers

1. The last sentence of the fourth paragraph provides further details about the first time Lian noticed a possible theft and, therefore, belongs in the second paragraph.

2. There may be a problem with employee theft during the evening shift from Monday through Thursday.

Reflect

Answers should include a discussion of the details and organization of both examples. The first example is more effective because it presents detailed information in an organized way. The second example does not identify when the items were suspected of being stolen, and it has some problems in organization. Lian's explanation for omitting the name of the coworker would work better in either the first paragraph or the last paragraph. The details about the hairbrush and headband belong in the second paragraph, not in the last paragraph.

On Your Own

See Writing Rubric on page 150

Scenario A

Purpose: To explain the risks and potential problems created by employees' smartphone use

Audience: Supervisor

The note should include **details** about the guards' use of smartphones and the potential safety risks. The employee could **organize** the message in a few brief paragraphs. The first paragraph should state the employee's purpose. Then the employee could describe what he or she has seen and discuss the possible consequences. If details are numerous, they could be organized in a bulleted or numbered list.

Scenario B

The employee's note should illustrate the concern by presenting **details** about customers' comments. It should also include details about how the sign could be changed or removed. The note could be **organized** in one or two brief paragraphs, stating the concern, explaining it in detail, and suggesting the change.

Scenario C

The employee should present **details** demonstrating that coworkers may be completing time sheets inaccurately, as well as details about the employee's suggestion. It is not necessary to name any coworkers; the employee's supervisor can decide whether to follow up. The employee could express the concern in a note or an e-mail. The employee should **organize** the writing in one or two brief paragraphs, stating the concern, explaining it in detail, and suggesting the change.

Scenario D

The note should present **details** about the problem and identify a solution, such as replacing the one door with two that open in one direction only. The note could be **organized** in one or two paragraphs. If multiple incidents are detailed, the organization could include a bulleted or numbered list.

Lesson 9 (pp. 56–61)

Skill Examples

1. D   **2.** J   **3.** C   **4.** G

Think About It

Example 1 is more effective. <u>ORGANIZATION:</u> In *Example 1*, Randy first presents specific information about Sanjay's strengths and then reviews his weaknesses. This information serves to clarify Randy's overall assessment of Sanjay's performance. The organization of *Example 2* is less clear, and provides less useful information about Sanjay's work. It begins as an evaluation, outlining some of Sanjay's strengths, but it shifts topic and becomes a commentary on the manufacturing department. <u>DETAILS:</u> *Example 1* provides an evaluation for most aspects of the job and includes a specific percentage of volume for comparison to the capacity of other workers. *Example 2* provides limited information about Sanjay's strengths and fails to include any details about areas needing improvement. In addition, unnecessary details about the manufacturing department are included.

Try It Out!

Possible Answers

1. Only the first two sentences are relevant.

2. When someone calls with a complaint, I usually write it down on a sticky note. This can create problems, so I suggest that we establish an official process.

Reflect

Answers should include a discussion of each writer's choices about details and organization. The first example is more effective. It is organized with section headings and provides the specific details requested. The second example includes irrelevant details and makes no use of headings, lists, or bullet points.

On Your Own

See Writing Rubric on page 150

Scenario A

Purpose: To summarize suggestions for handling misdirected calls

Audience: Supervisor

The report could be **organized** with section headings—for example, a summary heading and a heading for reporting procedures. A bullet point could be used for each procedure. The report should state why a clarification of procedures is necessary. The **details** should provide specifics about the different reporting procedures.

Scenario B

The report could be **organized** into three sections with these headings: summary, strengths, and weaknesses. The latter two sections should include specific **details** about the employee's strengths (attitude, professionalism) and weaknesses (disorganization).

Scenario C

The report could **organize** complaints into categories with appropriate section headings, such as "Unsafe Driving," "Late Deliveries," and "Damaged Goods." Additionally, the employee should use a consistent order to list specific information, such as by vehicle number or customer. The report should include all relevant **details**.

Scenario D

The report could be **organized** in three paragraphs. For example, it could include a short introductory paragraph stating the problem, a paragraph describing ways to make employees feel appreciated, and a paragraph describing ways to make them feel respected. The second and third paragraphs should include specific **details** rather than generalities.

Lesson 10 (pp. 62–67)

Skill Examples

1. D   2. J   3. C   4. G

Think About It

Example 1 is more effective. <u>DETAILS:</u> In *Example 1*, Faye provides specific details about office recycling and how it might benefit the company. *Example 2* is weaker because it provides fewer specific details. It also includes an irrelevant detail—the point about the office plants. <u>AUDIENCE:</u> In *Example 1*, Faye identifies a benefit of the program that would be persuasive to the audience (saving money). She also lets her reader decide if the idea is worth pursuing. *Example 2* does not explain how this could benefit the audience. The pushy tone could also be off-putting to the audience.

Try It Out!

Possible Answers

1. They would not have to turn customers away.

2. Since dogs such as pit bulls and Dobermans require extra training, the request for dog-training sessions has nearly doubled.

Reflect

Answers should focus on details that were included or could be added to make each proposal appealing to the audience. The first example contains the information the audience needs to evaluate the proposal, including details about the current training and the proposed training. The example also points out how the training could benefit the company by increasing efficiency and reducing legal risks. The second example explains the problem and solution but does not clearly identify possible benefits.

On Your Own

See Writing Rubric on page 150

Scenario A

Topic: Neatness of waiting room

Purpose: To propose an afternoon cleaning plan for the waiting room

The e-mail should include **details** about the untidiness, along with detailed steps explaining the proposed cleaning plan. The employee could appeal to the **audience's** interests by discussing the benefits of cleaning in the afternoon. To ensure **clarity**, the e-mail should address the details listed above and provide additional information the manager might need, such as who will be responsible for cleaning.

Scenario B

The letter should include **details** about the electronic signature pads and the potential advantages of having messengers use them. The **audience** is likely to be concerned with employee efficiency as well as budget costs. To ensure **clarity**, the employee should briefly describe the electronic signature pad and how it works.

Scenario C

The employee should present **details** illustrating the need for the company to provide protective clothing, sunscreen, and insect repellent. These details could include information about the safety risks as well as the expenses employees are incurring by providing these items themselves. The **audience** is more likely to provide the requested items if the employee can demonstrate that the current procedure is unsafe or prohibitively expensive for employees. Including the details listed above and organizing the message logically will help ensure its **clarity**.

Scenario D

The employee's proposal should present **details** to show why hiring additional meat cutters would benefit the plant. The proposal could be organized into a few brief paragraphs or presented as a report with several short sections. To ensure that the **audience** finds the proposal persuasive, the employee should stress how this would benefit the company by improving safety, morale, and product quality. To ensure **clarity**, the employee should provide specific information about problems caused by the staffing shortage.

Lesson 11 (pp. 70–75)

Skill Examples

1. D   2. K   3. B   4. H

Think About It

Example 2 is more effective. FORMAT: The notice in *Example 2* will reach a wider audience. It will communicate information to existing customers as well as potential customers. The notice in *Example 1* will be seen only by existing customers. DETAILS: *Example 2* includes important details, such as when the new services will be available and what specific items can be cleaned. *Example 1* is missing some of these details—most notably, when services will be available.

Try It Out!

Possible Answers

1. Joey could have included the date the increased prices will go into effect and the amount of the delivery increase.

2. We will continue to use the highest quality ingredients because you deserve the best.

Reflect

Answers should discuss the choice of details included and the clarity of each message. *Example 1* includes details about the increased charges and how the increase is related to rising fuel costs. *Example 2* omits specific details about when the increases will go into effect and how much the charge for delivery will increase. All points in *Example 1* are clearly stated, while the connection between the last two sentences in *Example 2* could be clearer.

On Your Own

See Writing Rubric on page 150

Scenario A

Purpose: To inform customers about the bakery's move and grand opening

Format: Notice

The **format** should be a notice that can be easily mailed. The notice should include key **details**, such as the new address, the date of the opening, and the free coffee, and explain the positive points about the new location **clearly**.

Scenario B

A business letter is an appropriate **format** for this communication. It is essential to accurately note the key **details**, such as when the new policy begins and the acceptable time frame for payments. The letter should also explain **clearly** that services will be withheld if payments are late.

Scenario C

Since the information can be summed up briefly, a letter or mailed notice would be an effective **format**. The communication should include all the **details** about the extended hours and present them **clearly.**

Scenario D

A business letter or a mailed notice would be effective **formats** for this communication. The message should include **details** about when Dr. Garcia is retiring and Dr. Leibowitz's availability and credentials. It should also **clearly** specify how patients can transfer their care to Dr. Leibowitz or another doctor.

Lesson 12 (pp. 76–81)

Skill Examples

1. E   2. F   3. E   4. K

Think About It

Example 2 is more effective. DETAILS: *Example 2* includes the necessary details of the customer's complaint, as well as what the company is doing to investigate the complaint. This helps reassure the customer that the complaint is being taken seriously. In contrast, *Example 1* is lacking in sufficient detail. <u>CLARITY:</u> *Example 1* uses vague phrases like *and such* and *or something*. This may lead the reader to wonder whether the writer understands the problem. In *Example 2*, the writer uses specific details to describe the problem and its likely cause. The writer also indicates the next steps in resolving the problem.

Try It Out!
Possible Answers

1. *stuff, What can I say, These things happen, slack off a little, this is just how it goes*

2. We will make it up to you by providing your next scheduled day of cleaning services free of charge.

Reflect
Answers should discuss the relevance and adequacy of details included, the clarity of the writing, and the appropriateness of the tone. Both writers apologize for the problem and ask for more details about it. However, the first example is more effective since it includes sufficient details to show an understanding of the problem, explains the next steps clearly, and has a polite, sympathetic tone. The second example does not include enough details of how the writer will make up for the poor service. The language is also too informal for a business communication.

On Your Own
See Writing Rubric on page 150

Scenario A
Purpose: To obtain additional details about the problem and assure the customer that the company will help resolve it

Audience: Customer

The e-mail should include **details** restating the customer's complaint, asking for any additional information needed, and suggesting a course of action, such as sending a technician out to do repairs. The e-mail should be **clear** about the information the writer needs and the next steps the company will take. The **tone** should be sympathetic and professional.

Scenario B
The e-mail should include **details** about the specific information needed, such as the customer's contact information, the item purchased, and the date of the purchase. It should also explain that this information will be forwarded to the manager. The e-mail should **clearly** explain what the company will do next to address the problem. The e-mail should have a polite and professional **tone.**

Scenario C
The response should include **details** about the complaint, such as the date and time the technician was scheduled to arrive, as well as details about when the company will contact the customer to reschedule. The response should **clearly** explain what information is needed and when the customer can expect to hear from a representative. The **tone** should be reassuring and professional.

Scenario D
The response should include **details** about the two problems the customer mentioned, what the carpenter can do to resolve them, and what the customer should do to help resolve them. The response should **clearly** explain that the carpenter is responsible for the scratch and will fix it for free, but that the sticky hinge is probably a manufacturing defect. The response should have an apologetic and professional **tone.**

Lesson 13 (pp. 82–87)

Skill Examples
1. A   2. F   3. C   4. J

Think About It
Example 2 is more effective. <u>TONE:</u> *Example 2* is written in a formal and more professional tone. It mentions the discussions that took place at the meeting and informs the recipients of what supplies Krager Medical Supply offers them. In addition, it provides a contact number for Paula. This makes it easier to contact her. <u>CLARITY:</u> By including specific information about the meeting and the hospital's needs, *Example 2* clearly shows how the company can help meet those needs. In contrast, *Example 1* is a generic form letter that does not clearly show that the company understands the hospital's needs.

Try It Out!
Possible Answers

1. Cherie should have explained that she is writing to thank the customer.

2. Thank you again for your e-mail. I truly appreciate your kind words about my customer service skills. Sincerely,

Reflect
Answers should discuss the effectiveness of the chosen formats, the tone of each message, and the clarity of each message. Brief formats, such as a note or an e-mail, are appropriate choices for these writers' purposes. The first example is somewhat clearer and uses an appropriately warm but professional tone. The second message is slightly less clear. Parts of the letter, such as the comment about doing somersaults, are overly informal for a communication with a customer.

On Your Own

See Writing Rubric on page 150

Scenario A

Purpose: To advertise Customer Appreciation Day

Audience: Current and potential customers

The **tone** of the message should be enthusiastic and appreciative of customers. The best **format**, as Lena requests, is a notice on the company's website. Different type sizes, font styles, and bullet points should be used to highlight and organize the details. To ensure that the message is **clear**, it should contain all the specific details that Lena mentioned.

Scenario B

The **tone** of the letter should be warm and professional. Because the writer is communicating directly with a supervisor, it is not necessary to use the business letter **format**. A less formal format, such as a note, a letter, or an e-mail, would be appropriate. To ensure that the letter **clearly** communicates the writer's appreciation, it should include specific information about Seantrell's attributes, such as his skill and work ethic.

Scenario C

The **tone** of the postcard should be friendly but professional. Within the postcard **format**, the writer should use techniques such as bold type or capitalization to emphasize the most important parts of the message. This will help ensure that the main idea of the communication is **clear** to its recipients.

Scenario D

The **tone** of the letter should be warm and professional but not overly formal. It would be appropriate to include a memory or detail about the writer's relationship with the patient. A thank you card is an appropriate **format** in cases involving a friendly relationship. To ensure that the letter **clearly** expresses the writer's gratitude, it should mention the specific gift and why this gift is appreciated.

Lesson 14 (pp. 88–93)

Skill Examples

1. D   2. K   3. C   4. H

Think About It

Example 2 is more effective. <u>DETAILS:</u> *Example 2* includes most of the details the client needs to understand the invoice and payment procedures. *Example 1* is less specific. It lists specific items and services but leaves out prices and quantities. <u>TONE:</u> The tone of *Example 1* is overly harsh, due to the excessive use of capital letters and the lack of words such as *please*. *Example 2* uses appropriately polite, professional language while still conveying information clearly.

Try It Out!

Possible Answers

1. Please look over all of the charges in the itemized bill.

2. This is a reminder that your payment of _____ is overdue.

Reflect

Answers should discuss the details included in each example, as well as the organization and tone of the examples. The first example is more effective since it includes a list of specific charges, uses a formal and professional tone throughout, and presents information in a logical order. The second example refers to an attachment that provides adequate details. However, this example is less effective since some of the language is too casual, and one sentence is out of order.

On Your Own

See Writing Rubric on page 150

Scenario A

Purpose: To explain the payment details

Audience: Clients (Mr. and Mrs. Michaels)

The letter should include **details** about the types of payment that are accepted and when the payment is due. Paragraph breaks could be used to **organize** the letter, with the first paragraph introducing the attached notice of payment and the second paragraph providing payment details. The format should be a business letter, and the **tone** should be formal and professional.

Scenario B

The **details** in the letter should include the total days and hours worked, the amount paid, and the amount owed. It would also be appropriate to explain how the error likely occurred. Paragraph breaks could be used to **organize** these ideas, and one paragraph should list in order the weeks and weekend days worked. The **tone** should be professional but understanding since this was probably a simple oversight on the employer's part.

Scenario C

The letter should include **details** about the payment due date, cost of labor, number of hours billed, and total charges. Paragraph breaks could be used to **organize** these ideas. Since the payment is late, the **tone** should be serious but not angry.

Scenario D

The letter should discuss the **details** included in the invoice, particularly any points that might be unfamiliar to the client, such as how the roofer charges for different materials used, and how much material was needed to repair that section of the roof. The letter should be **organized** in paragraphs, first stating the overall charges and then explaining the specifics. The **tone** should be friendly and helpful.

Lesson 15 (pp. 96–101)

Skill Examples
1. D   2. K   3. B   4. F

Think About It
Example 2 is more effective. <u>ORGANIZATION:</u> *Example 1* is organized in paragraph form, which makes it difficult for the reader to easily identify all of the questions. *Example 2* uses headings and bullet points, which make it easy to read. <u>CLARITY:</u> If the questions are unclear, the sales representative might give the wrong information.

Try It Out!
Possible Answers
1. Kirk's purpose is to get the date of delivery, so he should ask about that in the first paragraph.
2. This e-mail is in reference to the following parts I ordered online.

Reflect
Answers should include a discussion regarding whether each message is clear and well organized. The first example sticks to the relevant points and is clear. It includes bullet points to help organize the writer's questions. The second example fulfills the writer's purpose but could do so more effectively. A clearly stated purpose should be at the beginning of the message, and irrelevant details should not be included.

On Your Own
See Writing Rubric on page 150

Scenario A
Purpose: To learn more about products

Audience: Salesperson

The e-mail should include **clearly** worded questions that address the specific items available and their prices. It would be helpful to **organize** the e-mail using bullet points or paragraphs so that each question is apparent to the reader.

Scenario B
To ensure that the message is **clear**, all the relevant details should be stated, such as the writer's name, the items ordered, and the date of the order. A bulleted list of parts will help **organize** the message.

Scenario C
An effectively **organized** message would ask at the beginning why the bill is so much higher than in the previous year. To ensure that the message is **clear**,

the manager should directly state that she would like an explanation for the higher prices.

Scenario D
To ensure that the message is **clear**, the questions should be specific and ask about relevant topics, including available snack items, costs, and delivery schedules. These questions could be **organized** in a list with bullet points. Headings could be used if each topic has several questions.

Lesson 16 (pp. 102–107)

Skill Examples
1. E   2. F   3. E   4. K

Think About It
Example 2 is more effective. <u>CLARITY:</u> In *Example 2*, Michael explains exactly what he heard on the recording and why it was confusing to him. *Example 1* is weaker because Michael does not describe the recording in full. He states that it should be changed without explaining why. <u>TONE:</u> In *Example 2*, Michael's tone is friendly, which is appropriate when pointing out a minor problem like this one. The tone of *Example 1* is direct, which is not necessarily bad. However, Michael crosses the line into rudeness in his last paragraph, and this makes the entire message seem unfriendly and critical.

Try It Out!
Possible Answers
1. Jesse should describe the specific error he found rather than make general statements about the magazine publishing industry.
2. I would appreciate it if you would more carefully check for this kind of error in future issues of *United States History Magazine*. Thank you.

Reflect
Answers should discuss each message's details, clarity, and tone. Both examples include specific details; however, the first example states the problem more clearly and presents only the essential details. The second example presents too many irrelevant details and does not clearly state what the reader should do about the problem. The first example uses an appropriately respectful tone, while the second example conveys a condescending, superior attitude.

On Your Own

See Writing Rubric on page 150

Scenario A

Purpose: To inform webmaster of the broken link and the cause

Format: E-mail

The e-mail should include precise **details** about the page on which the problem is located, the link that is broken, and the likely cause of the problem. These details, along with a **clear** explanation of the problem, will help ensure that the reader understands the problem. The **tone** of the e-mail should be professional and respectful.

Scenario B

The letter should **clearly** state that the clerk is writing to praise the delivery company for providing excellent service. To make sure the right person gets credit, the letter should include accurate **details**, such as the shop's name, the driver's name, the date and time he assisted the clerk, and the specific actions he performed. The **tone** of the letter should be professional but warm and enthusiastic.

Scenario C

The letter should **clearly** state up front that the night manager was dissatisfied with the technical support. It should also clearly describe how the solution could have been given much more quickly. The letter should include **details** about the technical problem, whom the employee spoke with, and how many times the employee was put on hold. The **tone** should be polite, direct, and professional.

Scenario D

The letter should make **clear** that the employee thinks the security guards could do a better job keeping the mall safe. It should also show that the employee understands that he or she may not have enough information on what security guards should be doing. The letter should include **details** about the guards' specific actions, such as how often they talk with each other. The **tone** should be polite and professional.

Lesson 17 (pp. 108–113)

Skill Examples

1. E   **2.** H   **3.** B   **4.** J

Think About It

Example 2 is more effective. <u>DETAILS:</u> *Example 2* includes specific details about the topics of discussion and the time allotted for each topic. Lucia also provides her contact information and specific details about the location of the meeting. *Example 1* lists only vague descriptions of the meeting topics, and it

is missing important details about the meeting location, the organizer, and even the company whose product is being launched. <u>ORGANIZATION:</u> *Example 1* includes bullet points with general topics, but the agenda items are not listed in any particular order and do not include specific information. *Example 2* lists agenda items in chronological order. This helps attendees know exactly what will be discussed, when, and for how long.

Try It Out!

Possible Answers

1. The agenda should include the meeting's start and end times. This is particularly important because one of the participants will not be available during the afternoon.

2. **LOCATION:** Mr. Howell's office, Millennium Building, First Floor, Room 135B

Reflect

Answers should include a discussion of purpose, details, and organization. The first example clearly explains the purpose for the requested meeting in the first paragraph. The second example does not specifically identify the purpose. While both messages are clearly organized, Sarah should have included important details, such as the meeting location and the start and end times.

On Your Own

See Writing Rubric on page 150

Scenario A

Topic: Meeting about park construction

Format: E-mail

The e-mail should request two specific **details**: the length of the meeting and its location. The message should point out that the writer needs these details to confirm his or her availability. Since the content of the message is fairly brief, it can be **organized** in paragraph form.

Scenario B

The purpose of the message is to propose setting up a date to make a presentation. The message should include the most important **details** about the presentation and request information about any current school programs that teach children about nutrition. The message can be **organized** into two short paragraphs, one explaining why it is important to educate children about good nutrition and one with the presentation details.

Scenario C

The e-mail should include **details** about the specific discussion items the buyer wishes to add to the agenda—pricing and delivery. The e-mail can be

organized into two short paragraphs. One could confirm the proposed date, time, and location. The other could suggest the additional discussion items.

Scenario D

The e-mail should include **details** about the date and time the installer is available. The installer could even suggest more than one possibility; for example, "I can meet with you on Tuesday at 4:00 P.M. or on Thursday at 2:00 P.M." The e-mail can be **organized** into two short paragraphs. One could state that the installer is unavailable at the proposed time. The other could suggest one or more alternate dates and times.

Lesson 18 (pp. 114–119)

Skill Examples
1. B   2. J   3. C   4. K

Think About It

Example 1 is more effective. <u>DETAILS:</u> In *Example 1*, Manny includes specific details that help the reader understand more about pricing and delivery. He also points out that the delivery schedule allows time for updating the display. Details are lacking in *Example 2*. <u>ORGANIZATION:</u> In *Example 1*, Manny uses headings to indicate the main topics addressed. He uses bullets points to organize specific points. *Example 2* addresses several different topics within a single paragraph, which makes it much less organized.

Try It Out!

Possible Answers

1. John should specify which type of glass bead he is referring to.

2. Please understand that I am now working with higher quality, more costly materials, so I have had to raise my prices to stay in business.

Reflect

Answers should include a discussion of how clear each message is, whether it is sufficiently detailed, and how well it is organized. The first example is clearer because it restates the concerns mentioned in the original query. The second example makes good use of bullet points but would be more effective if transition words were used in the paragraphs.

On Your Own

See Writing Rubric on page 150

Scenario A

Topic: Freelancer's payment

Audience: Freelance writer

The e-mail should be **clear** about why the payment was delayed and when it will be sent. It should include **details** about the delay in processing tax forms and the anticipated two-week turnaround time. The e-mail could use two short paragraphs to **organize** these points. Transition words, such as *because* and *soon*, could also be used.

Scenario B

To ensure that the message is **clear**, it should briefly restate the issue and then present the requested information. It should include **details** about the store's location and the items ordered. These details can be **organized** using five lines, one for each empty space on the order form.

Scenario C

The response should **clearly** state the **details** regarding when the game will be released, where it can be purchased, and how many copies will be available. These details can be **organized** using bullet points. It would also be appropriate to use headings to organize information, such as *Release Date, Availability in Stores*, and *Initial Release*.

Scenario D

The response should **clearly** restate Jim's issue and give details about when the shipment will arrive. To ensure that there is no miscommunication, the response should include all the **details** of the shipment, such as the contents and the scheduled time and location of the delivery. It would also be helpful to include a few details about the cause of the delay. Paragraphs or bullet points can be used to **organize** the information.

Writing for Work Rubric

	1 (INEFFECTIVE)	3 (EFFECTIVE)	5 (HIGHLY EFFECTIVE)
Clarity	Thoughts and ideas may be confusing.	Thoughts and ideas are generally clear.	Thoughts and ideas are clear.
	Improper use of vocabulary makes meaning unclear.	Use of vocabulary is not perfect but does not cause confusion.	Precise use of vocabulary adds clarity.
	Improper use of transition words may be confusing.	Most transition words are used properly, but readers have to do a little work to connect ideas.	Transition words are helpful and precise.
	Readers may not be able to determine the purpose and the main idea.	The purpose and the main idea are fairly clear.	The purpose and the main idea are obvious.
Organization	Most ideas lack organization, are unrelated, or are out of sequence.	Most ideas are organized and properly sequenced, but connections between ideas are not always clear.	Ideas are organized, clear, properly sequenced, and logically connected.
	Structure is loose or random.	Structure is organized, but ideas sometimes go off topic.	Structure is organized, and ideas stay on topic.
	Writing is unfocused and difficult to follow.	Writing is generally focused but not always easy to follow.	Writing is focused and easy to follow.
Tone	Tone may lack maturity, consistency, or professionalism.	Tone is generally mature, consistent, and appropriately professional.	Tone is mature, consistent, and appropriately professional.
	It shows a lack of respect for the audience or topic.	It is mostly respectful to the audience and topic.	It is respectful to the audience and topic.
	It is too formal or too informal for the audience or topic.	It may be a bit too formal or informal.	It is appropriately formal or informal.
Details	Key details are missing.	Most of the key details are included.	All the important details are included.
	Many unimportant details are included.	Some unimportant details are included.	No unimportant details are included.
	Many details are unclear or inaccurate.	Some details are unclear or inaccurate.	Details are clear and accurate.
	Readers may be left with many questions.	Readers may be left with some questions.	Readers should have no unanswered questions.
Conventions -grammar -spelling -punctuation -sentence structure	Writing contains several errors in grammar, spelling, punctuation, or sentence structure. Errors make the message hard to read and understand.	Writing contains some errors in grammar, spelling, punctuation, or sentence structure. These errors usually do not affect meaning but could create disruption for readers.	Writing contains almost no errors in grammar, spelling, punctuation, or sentence structure.